WHAT I WISH I COULD TELL YOU

Stories, Poetry & Recipes

WHAT I WISH I COULD TELL YOU

Stories, Poetry & Recipes
Camden Writers

Waxing Crescent Press
Camden, SC

ISBN-13: 978-0692805510
ISBN-10: 0692805516

Printed in the United States of America

*Dedicated to all sojourners, pilgrims,
and vagabonds with stories to tell.*

There are things known and things unknown and in-between are the doors.

Jim Morrison

Contents

Living the Good Life

This Is the Day

Moving On

The Road Ahead

Is There a Cook in the House?

Preface

Two years ago, Camden Writers published *Serving Up Memory*, a collaborative work of stories, poems, photographs and recipes. We were not only pleased with the book's reception, but also surprised at its broad appeal. Although the selections were local and personal, they struck a chord: our memories, readers often told us, stirred their own. This reception inspired us to dish up a second serving.

What I Wish I Could Tell You shares its title with a poem included in these pages, because, after considering many titles, our common theme seemed to echo the sense of longing expressed in those words. Our aim in this anthology is to use our voices and our stories to say what—and *who*—we remember, what has touched us, grieved us or given us joy.

This anthology comes from our hearts and we hope it speaks to yours.

The Editors

For some of us, books are as important as almost anything else on Earth. What a miracle it is that out of these small, flat, rigid squares of paper unfolds world after world after world, worlds that sing to you, comfort and quiet or excite you. Books help us understand who we are and how we are to behave. They show us what community and friendship mean; they show us how to live and die.

Anne Lamott, Bird by Bird:
Some Instructions on Writing and Life

Living the Good Life

There are only two ways to live your life. One is as though nothing is a miracle. The other is as though everything is a miracle.
Albert Einstein

Living the Good Life
Kathryn Etters Lovatt

J.E. Horton was a man who, if he knew you, or if he just knew *of* you, might show up at your door. Stooped a little from the six-foot-four of younger years, curved with a farmer's need to look long and deep at the particulars of his land, his powerful frame would still fill the doorframe.

J.E. Horton

More than once, he came by my house, sometimes alone, sometimes with his daughter Betty, once with granddaughter, Laurie Slade Funderburk, when she was campaigning for the South Carolina House of Representatives. Wherever J.E. went, family members frequently and happily tagged along.

"We wanted to bring you a few things from the garden," he'd say, a smile so broad even his signature pencil mustache turned up. "We thought y'all might enjoy them."

Produce spilled from his great arms. Forefront, he held tomatoes and cucumbers; beneath lay a foundation of corn. Silken tassels tumbled like strands of hair and wrapped his fingers. Whoever accompanied him that morning would stand slightly behind, holding the screen door ajar and cradling the surplus they had been assigned to carry.

"Goodness," I probably said, and I meant it.

Visits like this are a rare thing these days and times, but this generosity used to be the custom of people who kept substantial gardens. Folks loaded up their extras and went along to friends and neighbors. They shared their abundance and spread their plenty.

But J.E.'s bounty was not the prize, although prized it was—who doesn't want a cornucopia of vegetables picked not long before, the cool of a morning still rising off them? The real treasure was his gesture, a simple act of goodwill that said he'd thought of me. Or maybe he thought of you—my house was not the only one he visited on those occasions. He hardly took time to bring everything into the kitchen and pat my back before he needed to get along to his next stop.

Last October, a month shy of his ninety-sixth birthday, Jesse Ervin Horton Jr. passed away. I, like so many others, bowed my head at the news. To lose a man of such good cheer and benevolence strikes the heart a blow. He was missed this year at the Kershaw County Farmers' Market, an enterprise for which he campaigned and which he eagerly supported. He moved genially among the crowds there, weaving toward a familiar face, or he stayed put and let people come to him. We all wanted a word or two, our little moment. He gladly obliged, dispensing his small, sweet blessings every Saturday, spring to fall.

"Pop always took time to talk to anyone," Betty Slade said about her father. "Oh, he enjoyed people and fun." For guidance, Betty said, he relied on one humble imperative, The Golden Rule: *Do unto others as you would have them do unto you.*

"He loved his family, too," she added, "and we loved him back. We did everything together."

That included working the farm, one owned by his family since the early 1900s, when his parents established a dairy farm and planted their commercial acres in cotton. The youngest of nine children, J.E. was born there in the Shamokin Community, seven miles north of Camden's downtown post office, on November 24, 1919.

"He was born on the farm, born into farming, and he never left," said Betty. "He was born in a house that was later turned into the dairy barn."

J.E. and Betty

***

J.E.'s early years were spent living a country boy's life. His days were anchored in the daily tasks of raising crops and tending livestock, but summers also found him swimming in the creek; winters he and his siblings pulled raw potatoes from the potato hill for lunch before heading to the schoolhouse.

Growing up in fields and barns, he learned the nature of plants and trees, how to pour up feed and draw down milk. His boyhood taught him the value of rain and sun, the peril of late frosts or summer hailstorms. Success, he realized, as all dedicated farmers must, depended largely upon hard work and a deep-rooted belief that what is nurtured will ultimately prosper.

At his brother Henry's store in Dusty Bend, J.E. also came to recognize the worth of good company and a good laugh. During the many afternoons and weekends he worked at the grocery, he always got a kick out of customers bending over to pry up the quarter glued to the floor in front of the Coke machine. He stayed busy, at the farm and in the store.

J. E. and Sara

Then one day, Miss Sara Frances Burch caught his eye.

"Dad met Mom when she moved to Camden with family," Betty said. "Her dad—my granddaddy—helped start up Powe Veneer Plant in the middle 1930's. It was located in the area where *The Chronicle–Independent* and other businesses are now. The story goes that he saw Mom walk up the street where Williams' Gas Station sat across from the courthouse and was so taken aback by her beauty that he followed her and introduced himself. Undoubtedly, he swept her off her feet. Everyone says that Dad was a true Southern gentleman."

After J.E. and Sara wed in 1940, the young couple took over the dairy. For thirty-five dollars a month, they rented his parents' dairy cows. In a few years, even with a baby coming along, they saved enough to purchase a brand new bright yellow 1947 Chevrolet panel truck for $1,442.00. Until 1953, Sara delivered Horton Dairy's milk, cream and eggs. Milk cost twenty-five-cents a quart; eggs went for fifty-cents a dozen. Each morning, Sara, with the help of young boys in town like Boykin Roseborough and Dickie Tiller, picked up two three-hundred-pound blocks of ice from John Villipigue's ice house to keep her products cold.

Even while the dairy was in operation, J.E. ran a logging outfit. He started out with a mule and an iron wagon, but soon traded in his mule and some cash for a tractor. He employed up to ten men. Larry Slade recalled his father-in-law's stories about logging the cypress out of Goodale State Park when it was still known as Adam's Mill Pond.

"He used mules and handsaws," said Larry. "They would go to the sawmill with a load of trees and come out with slats—logs with bark on one side and cut wood on the other—to lay on the roadway so they could drive a truck down to pick up more logs without getting stuck."

"You need a lot of faith to farm," J.E. liked to say, but he confessed to Larry that his Alice Chalmers tractor, which had a habit of breaking down, taught him how to cuss.

In 1947, J.E. bought a piece of equipment called, ironically, a Logger's Dream. Betty said her mother had a bad feeling about it from the start. When one of the machine's stanchions broke, a truck-load of logs rolled out on J.E.

"Most people never would have recovered," said Larry. "He ended up with pins in his arms and legs. He broke his foot, too, but the x-ray machine wasn't working when he first got there. By the time anybody realized what was going on, the bones had healed. They healed wrong, and the only thing the doctors could do was operate and re-break the bones. J.E. wasn't going to let them do that."

After a long stay in the hospital, J.E. went home, but he was pretty much put out of action for a year. His foot would give him trouble for the rest of his life. "It hurt him," said Larry, "and it threw him off. He was always sticking stuff in his shoe to help him keep his balance."

Once back on his feet, J.E. returned to logging and ran the operation until 1950, when he took a job with DuPont in the power department. He stayed until his retirement in 1981.

A lot happened in those thirty-plus swing-shift years: J.E. and Sara raised Betty; Betty met Larry. ("I'm going to be watching you," J.E. warned Larry when things with him and Betty turned serious.) Betty and Larry married and had their own children, Robert and Laurie, "the light of their grandparents' lives," said Betty. All of them grew up witnessing how a farm works and how much work it takes to farm.

In his spare time, whenever that might have been, J.E. continued to cruise timber for logging companies, estimating how many board feet a tract would bring and tallying a market price. Betty said all he had to do was look up and across the trees to nail the numbers.

He closed the dairy, but not to spare himself labor. He began raising beef cattle.

Moving her grandfather's cows from one field to another was always a family activity, Laurie said. "Whoever was around was obliged to grab a small branch or broomstick and to stop any wayward cow from wandering off."

Two or three times a summer, when J.E. cut hay, his grandchildren helped load bales on the trailer and into the barn. "It was really hard work for little kids," said Robert. "I was so happy when Papa switched from small bales to large bales because large bales were moved with a tractor."

Robert also recalled adventures on many of the Saturdays he was in elementary school. "Papa would take me with him to farm auctions. We drove all over to attend these 'sales' as he called them." Those long drives, with J.E. at the wheel and his grandson reading the map, served as good opportunities to offer a few words of guidance.

"One of Papa's talking points was the importance of not being a 'hothead,'" Robert said. "He thought it very unbecoming for person to lose his or her temper and risk looking 'like a fool.'" Later in life, J.E. would talk to him about the stock market. He preached long and hard about the value of "sleeping money."

J.E. was a little superstitious too, a fact brought home to Robert when he was in middle school and being treated by a doctor for a plantar wart on his right foot. His grandfather drove him deep in the woods. "We got out and walked around and looked for some time until we found an animal bone. He had me take off my sock and shoe and rub the bone on the wart. He then had me throw the bone over my left shoulder." J.E. instructed Robert not to look back. "A few weeks later he heard me say that the wart was gone. He said, 'I told you the bone remedy would work.'"

J.E. and Sara eagerly took a role in raising their grandchildren.

"Our grandmother picked us up from school through my freshman year. She took us to piano lessons, soccer, baseball," said Robert. "If we had nothing else to do, we went to their house. Our parents met us there for supper and then we went home. This was the routine we followed every day. In the summers, Laurie and I basically lived at our grandparents' house."

The J.E. Hortons were married nearly fifty-five years when Sara died April 14, 1994. Retired by then for a decade from DuPont, J.E. had his family to help him through his wife's loss, and he had the farm, which never ran short of things that needed doing. Work was good medicine.

"Daddy kept up with everything—news, politics, the latest in agriculture," Betty explained. "He loved drafting. And he dearly loved to watch Westerns and to read, especially medical journals and medical books."

J.E.'s interest in studying health was initiated by his role as caretaker not only for Sara but also for his sister, Jessie. "He got to be an expert," said Betty. "Everybody in the family called him Dr. Horton."

Her father also became a regular at S. C. Philharmonic concerts. Until he married and moved to Georgia, his grandson Robert was principal bass trombonist for the orchestra.

"Pop would put on his suit, shine his shoes, and trim his mustache. He really enjoyed the music and the friends he met at The Koger Center and, of course, he loved seeing his grandson in his tux. Pop's niece, Margie Workman Gay, daughter of his sister Pearl, also would join the family for the concerts. A good time was had by all!"

Betty took a breath. "I could go on and on," she said. "Pop was never much of a rocker, if you know what I mean, he was a doer."

And patriarch to a family of doers.

In 2005, three generations of the J.E. Horton family accepted the Agri-Business Award of the year. J.E., a spry eighty-five at the time, still farmed, ran beef and logged. He would continue to keep a hand in these pursuits throughout his long life.

"I think living close to the land must keep you young," Laurie Slade Funderburk said of her grandfather at the awards ceremony.

J.E. had a lot of famous sayings—mostly advice. Everyone in the family has a favorite. Among them:

If you're going to do something, do it right.

You've got to help the working man.

Buy Made in America.

Be honest.

Never drive your best car to make a deal.

When saying goodbye, Laurie remembered, he would always end with *Be good to yourself.* That included eating well.

A fan of blueberries and probiotics, he believed in regular doses of cabbage and sweet potatoes, rutabagas and collard greens.

"Papa always liked to keep a pan of baked sweet potatoes in the peel on hand," said Laurie. "He also liked to cut up a rutabaga into small pieces—a dangerous job—and boil them in a pot."

J.E. heartily approved of his granddaughter running for office. Betty always heard the stories of how her own grandfather plowed in a necktie so he would be ready if any local politicians drove by and hollered for him to come along.

"Papa loved that I was in politics," said Laurie. "I inherited my Democrat values from him. He was always up for an adventure—a ride, going to see a relative or an old friend. Like his father before him, he didn't meet a stranger and could talk to anyone. That is a trait my mom cannot deny either."

When Laurie was in a race, J.E. made a list of friends and relatives and called them up. He went with her to knock on doors and pass out cards and bumper stickers. He handed out a few vegetables, too; some he put in paper bags with a campaign sticker attached to the front of them.

"Whether I was opposed or unopposed," she remembered, "he would put his hand on the shoulder of someone he just met or someone he hadn't seen in a long time and proudly tell them I was his granddaughter and to vote for me if they ever saw my name on the ballot. Sometimes I was around when he did this and while it was a little embarrassing, I let him do it because he loved it—and he loved me."

"His love of family and friends was evident," stressed Betty. "He believed in being honest and treating everybody with respect. As head of our family, he always led in prayer at all times and his prayers were very special, always personal."

J.E. was deeply committed to his church community at First Baptist, where he celebrated his ninetieth birthday to a full house, evidence of how many of us he gathered up and tucked beneath a wing. His voice strong and true, no artifice about him, he thanked God for every person who joined him on that special day.

He was grateful for his blessings, family first and foremost, including his great grandchildren—Slade, Jonathan, Matthew and Burch. J.E. rejoiced in their arrivals. Quick as he could get them loaded up, they came in prams or toddling to the farmers' market. He wanted them to see first-hand what the earth could yield and the fun of celebrating with friends. He believed in people the way he had faith in the land, that seeds sown and watered would come to harvest. That philosophy seemed to work like self-fulfilling prophecy.

The psychologist Abraham Maslow once said, "The great lesson is that the sacred is in the ordinary. That it is to be found in one's daily life, in one's neighbors, friends and family, in one's backyard."

J.E. Horton was a shining example of Maslow's tenet. It seemed in all those lone hours learning about nature combined with close time he spent with friends and family, he'd worked something out, deep inside, about who he was and how he would walk in the world. That decision lit his way, and always when he passed by, it cast an uncommon glow.

95th Birthday Celebration

Megan Anne Bevan's Poetry
Brenda Bevan Remmes

The oldest in my family, I was Megan's sister, babysitter, and defender against any sibling attacks. I remember when she turned forty someone asked her what was the hardest part of being the youngest. She said, "Watching my brother and sisters grow older knowing one day they will die and I will be left alone." I find it sadly ironic that Megan would be the one to leave us first.

Megan wrote throughout her life, although I knew little about her high school and college years, since I left home when she was only seven. Following college, she secured a job with *National Geographic Magazine,* and we all started to pay more attention. By the time she was forty-four, she was Vice-President of National Geographic Broadcast and Syndicated Series.

She loved Las Vegas and especially shooting dice. When she was diagnosed with a rare form of cancer, she said her chances at the craps table were better than her chances of staying alive, so she was bound to win at one of them. We were all heart-broken when she lost at life.

As is often the case when a loved-one dies, we packed up her belongings and stored them, unable to discard the many reminders that bound her to us. Not long ago while helping my mother clean out an upstairs closet, my sister found a box of Megan's high school mementoes. Included were a number of papers and poems written for one of her language-arts classes. What amazes me is not that she had written some fine pieces, but that she'd done so when she was seventeen years old. I'm sure if she were alive she's reprimand me and say, "Oh, Brenda, those were so NOT good." I tend to disagree and in her memory share two examples of her early poetry that keep her in our hearts today. The first, "Southern Heritage," follows this introduction. "Summer" is found later in this anthology.

Southern Heritage

Megan Bevan
1958-2004

The coming of black night
peering into the trees beyond the window,
gentle, steady November wind
blowing tails of Spanish moss—
Southern gentlemen's swaying beards.

Filled with spirits,
faces of the forgotten through the screen
of moss and limbs,
my reflection in their moist eyes.
Scent of magnolia.

Standing by the window,
feeling the breeze,
waiting for the night to erase
shadows in the trees,
thinking of days past.

How lovely to have sat on the veranda
and watched the view of the woods.

Spirits outside the window,
outlasting chilled December,
dancing into the night, leading me into the past
when this house filled with people—
gallant, romantic, Southern.

Shake away these haunting images—
Yesterdays.
Grandmother's voice,
Grandmother's dinner,
Blossom serving biscuits.

And through the divided light of the chandelier
spirits dancing from the lawn to the porch
to the dining room
take their places on either side
of the rosewood table.

Emma Marie Laubscher, born in Dow City, Iowa, in 1910, was widowed as a young mother in 1953. Three excerpts from a book written in her memory are included in this anthology. The book was authored by Brenda Bevan Remmes; however, it was written in the voice of Emma's youngest son, Bill, Brenda's husband.

Coming to America

Brenda Bevan Remmes (as told to her by her husband Bill)

The Remmes family wasn't poor by local standards. The Midwest during the 1800s was a place that was thirsting for settlers to farm the land and build the economy. On October 5, 1870, an article appeared in the *Denison Review* that announced, "A dozen new German arrivals were spotted coming up from the depot which adds so many more to the population of Crawford County, Iowa. The Germans are one of the most industrious and frugal class of people on the face of the earth and Crawford County is one of the most fortunate counties in the state in securing a German settlement within its borders."

In reality so many Germans came that by 1879 there was a newspaper written in German, *Die Denison Zeitung,* and a German Society was launched to promote culture. The Germans built an opera house along with a Methodist Church. Of course, all that enthusiasm would collapse with the onslaught of World War I, but when Grandmother and Grandfather Remmes arrived in this country, they were welcomed.

John Kasper Remmes and Anne Kuper were married in July of 1885 at St. Patrick's Catholic Church in Neola, Iowa. They remained devout Catholics throughout their lives. John emigrated along with one other family member from Hanover, Germany, in 1880 when he was twenty-four years old. Just for perspective, a year later James S. Garfield, the twentieth President of the United States was assassinated, and a year after that Jesse James was killed. The Wild West was beginning to be tamed, so they said.

Anne Kuper emigrated with her parents from the Dutch town of Zangberg in Dourn County in 1877 when she was thirteen years old. The 1920 County Plats of Crawford County showed that John K. and Anne Remmes owned 240 acres of land. I've been told that my grandfather purchased this land on a privately backed loan from a man in New Jersey. The land had originally belonged to the Sac and Fox Indian Nations. An accounting of land sales in Denison, Iowa, described how Jesse W. Denison of Rhode Island raised $51,000 to buy up tracts of land that had been offered by the US Government to Veterans of the War of 1812. Jesse

John Kasper and Anne Kuper Remmes

Denison built himself a house and called it a town in his honor. He then sold off tracts to immigrants. After my grandfather and grandmother's deaths, the loan was called in, and my father and his brothers lost it all.

I don't think my father and his brothers were bad farmers. They loved farming and they loved being a part of a big family. In fact, they loved being together so much, that I can't remember a time before my father's death that there weren't aunts and uncles living in the same house with us. Some say that's why a few of them stayed single—they weren't willing to give up the family meals and the readily available partners for a game of Pinochle, Pitch, or Uker. There was the drinking, too....good German beer. Drinking was so acceptable that the taverns kept their backdoors open on Sunday after church so that the congregation members could stop on the way home to pick up a few bottles to have after Sunday lunch. I remember stopping every week.

That big extended family all living in the same place pushed our mother to the brink on more than one occasion. My sister Betty remembers when she was only three that Mom packed up and took her to Wisconsin. Mom worked someplace, but Betty can't remember exactly what she did. Betty pleaded with Mom to go back to Iowa, and Dad wrote weekly begging her to come home. Finally, she did. She'd made her wedding vows in the Catholic Church and she took them seriously.

When they returned they moved into a tenant house with Sam

Fox and his daughter, Maxine. Sam was an indentured servant who had come to the USA agreeing that he'd work in exchange for the cost of transportation. Emma and Hank had two of the upstairs rooms to themselves in a house that had a half-mile lane that led to the main dirt road and a one-room schoolhouse.

The Remmes brothers pooled their money and rented farm land and things got some better, but there was still friction between my mom and my dad over the liberties that she felt his family members took. She was a penny-pincher who abhorred debt, lived frugally and padded their income with homegrown fruits, vegetables and a flock of chickens. The Remmeses had a tendency to show up for Sunday lunch and eat her whole week's budget of groceries in one afternoon.

My life revolved around Mom. She was a gutsy little thing, just over five feet, and only later did my sister and brother and I realize the risks she took to make our lives better than hers. Our dad encouraged us, but our mom was the one with the backbone and persistence to get things done. That's why we wanted to put something in writing, so that her grandchildren and great-grandchildren will know. She died

Emma Marie Remmes

too young—way before she could see the results that her sacrifices meant to others. Her offspring have succeeded beyond her wildest dreams. She'd claim bragging rights on each of them if she were still alive.

My mom, Emma Marie, grew up down the road from the Remmes farm, the next farm over. Biggest difference between her and Dad was their age. Dad was sixteen years older, so for the better part of his early years he was looking at other women. When she was starting elementary school, Dad had already signed up to fight in the war-to-end-all-wars. He didn't stay with the army long, though. A cook accidently dumped lye, instead of salt, into a pot of soup and several men became critically ill. Dad got an early discharge. He suffered from stomach problems all the rest of his life and died forty years later from stomach cancer.

Mom's mom and dad both emigrated from Switzerland at different times. Grandpa Fritz Laubscher came with his two brothers in March of 1907. He'd recount that he arrived at Ellis Island with only thirty-eight dollars in his pocket, but thirty-eight dollars at that time was the equivalent of $950 today, so he wasn't as bad off as he liked to pretend.

My grandmother, Marie Feller, arrived at Ellis Island in 1905 when she was fifteen with her sister and Uncle John Hasler. She told us her mother had a houseful of children and a derelict father who had abandoned them. When her Uncle John offered to take the two oldest girls to help with a boarding house he'd started in Sugarcreek, Ohio, her mother jumped at the opportunity. Marie was only lukewarm to the idea. She missed her family terribly throughout all the years she lived in Iowa.

Marie's sister, Lena, met Fritz's brother, Karl, and moved to Crawford County, Iowa. Then she introduced Marie to Fritz and the two sisters ended up marrying two brothers. That's maybe the biggest reason people say all the Laubschers look alike.

Grandmother and Grandfather Laubscher were married on December 11, 1909, at the German Methodist Episcopal Church. I have their wedding certificate. It's in German. Fritz was twenty-five, Marie was nineteen. Fritz farmed with his brother for a while, and ten years later they had saved enough to buy 202 acres of farming land of their own.

Mostly I remember Grandpa and Grandma Laubscher and their farm. After Dad died we moved into town, and the farm was where we went to either work or visit. Despite Mom's and Grandpa's occasional disagreements—and I am told they had some big ones—her sisters say Mom was his favorite.

The first thing Mom and her dad disagreed on was whether or not she would remain in school. The local one-room school took students through eighth grade. Mom wasn't that good of a student. Swiss German (Schweizer-Deutsch) was the only language spoken in her home and she struggled with English. Other students teased her and once the war broke out they made sarcastic remarks about her accent and told her to go back to Germany. Her father was incensed that the locals weren't intelligent enough to know the difference between German and Swiss. A law was passed making it illegal to speak German in public places and from then on the family focused harder on speaking English at home.

There were younger children to take care of and a farm to run. In the early part of the 1900s parents expected their children to work the farms and factories with them. The money that children made helped to support a family. Grandpa was of like-mind and he worked his children as if they were farm hands. He needed Emma at home.

Hank and Emma Remmes

At some point in her life, Mom began to realize what opportunities she'd missed by not staying in school. My brother and sister and I have discussed when that moment first began. Perhaps not this young, but at some time Mom realized she was smart enough to have gotten better jobs if she'd had more education and she decided her own children wouldn't make the same mistake.

In a small 3x5 inch notebook we found, Mom recorded a list of the people she'd worked for from the time she was eighteen until she married Dad. These were undoubtedly side-jobs she had to bring in some cash that probably included everything from housework, to caregiving, candling eggs, and fieldwork. Weeding beans and detasseling corn were unpaid chores that even Betty, John and I were expected to do. It was as natural to a farm kid as making your bed and brushing your teeth.

My mom and dad were married in the Catholic Church in Dunlap, Iowa. The marriage was not accepted graciously by her father and we can only speculate why. We just know there was a fight and Mom's youngest sister, Esther, was forbidden to attend. Over Grandpa's objections, Grandma Laubscher and Mom's oldest sister, Bertha, went anyway.

There are several reasons that may have caused Grandpa's disapproval: the first being the age difference between Mom and Dad and the second being his concern over the Catholic religion. Mom converted to Catholicism immediately and in the eyes of many ultimately became a better Catholic than Dad. Boy, can my brother, sister and I tell you stories about growing up Catholic in Denison, Iowa: parochial school, altar boys, weekly confession—the whole bit. While Grandpa and Grandma Laubscher remained with the Methodist Church, their faith was more lukewarm. It didn't hold the same leverage over their daily lives.

Perhaps the third and more prominent reason could have been Grandpa's financial analysis of what Hank Remmes had to offer

Emma. After the death of John Kasper Remmes in 1926, the farm next door had struggled.

At some point, the brothers invested in cattle and went to Colorado to pick them up and bring the herd back to Iowa, making them old-fashioned cowboys, I guess—good enough to move the cattle, but not good enough to keep them alive. The cattle got sick and died and the Remmes brothers were unable to control the debt. After their mother's death, the farm was sold off and the brothers tried tenant farming in an effort to hold things together.

Fritz Laubscher was undoubtedly not impressed. A man who had been frugal with his own money and always invested cautiously, he may have anticipated the hard times that would eventually be forced upon his oldest daughter. Emma had proven to be a worker and a devoted daughter and he depended on her to be there for him and Marie in case of sickness or death. Like many a reluctant father, he wasn't yet ready to give her away to another man.

The Pioneering Spirit
Kathryn Etters Lovatt

Southeastern Montana's High Plateau spreads far and wide, immense as a somber ocean at world's end. When the high plains reach the horizon, they merge into the famous sky, made bluer by contrast with the terrain's brooding palette. To my Southern eye, this first glimpse was a dizzying sight. Void of lush vines and stretches of forests or any verdant thing I could name, this domain belonged to the coulees, arroyos and washes that long ago laid claim to pieces of the West.

Marian Murphy Lovatt

The ground appeared to produce mostly hard dirt and tumbleweeds; the only crops I could see were roadside sage and greasewood, creosote, jags of cactus. Occasionally, a surprising oasis of massive trees slipped into view. Cottonwoods know water like a divining rod and cast their deep spreading roots by any reliable trickle.

They subsist on snowmelt and despite a scarcity of rain, breed and grow in gnarly stands.

In this cracked and fissured region, what flourishes must be able to survive searing heat, perilous cold and precious little moisture. But like winter, this frill-free terrain bears its own stark beauty. Before long, I learned to admire the fierce, if unfamiliar, landscape. In a similar way, this is how I came to appreciate my mother-in-law, whose solemn nature perfectly matched her native state.

The day before my wedding, Marian Murphy Lovatt flew South in practical black shoes, black pants, and a blouse that looked like all the others I would ever see her wear. A few dark strands still streaked her hair, turning the thick, short mass a deep shade of vintage pewter. She stood before me at attention: feet planted, shoulders squared, hands clasped at her back. A registered nurse, who served as a WAVE in the South Pacific during WWII, a military stance somehow suited her. Without a trace of a smile or a 'how-do-you-do,' she inspected me head-to-toe, deciding, I suppose, if I passed muster.

Daniel and Esther Murphy

Already in her seventies, she looked not so much her age as ageless, like she had been salted down and seasoned by the elements. A lifetime of glacial winds and harsh weather scored her skin until fine lines crisscrossed her face like roads on a well-used map. Unlike my own mother, who pampered her delicate skin and resented every wrinkle, Marian never grumbled about the signs of time. She knew better than to resist what couldn't be changed and saved her energy for what could. A highline ranch that backed up to the Missouri River Breaks surely helped shape her stoic character.

Dan Murphy, Marian's father, was only fourteen when he sailed out of Ireland and into the dream of an America on the cusp of the twentieth century. He worked his way from New York City westward, and once there, he became a genuine cowboy down to chaps and leather gauntlets. He rode the cattle trail out of Texas for the XIT brand, letters nearly impossible for rustlers to alter. When the government offered wild land in the Montana Territory to homesteaders, he married his sweetheart from back home, gathered his savings, and set out to stake a claim. A man who understood the value of water, he chose tracts with springs and branches and disregarded the borders of broken ground and badlands. Those he thought he could handle, and he did.

At its peak, the Murphy spread grazed 5,000 head of sheep on eight sections, or roughly 5,000 unconstrained acres. Once fences started going up in the mid-twenties, Murphy began to switch over to cattle and horses. No matter. There was work enough to go around for him and his wife, eight surviving offspring plus everybody in the bunkhouse, whether cowpokes or sheepherders.

Marian, the oldest girl, learned early to ride and roundup, to shear and brand. She came to know the amount of food required to sustain men on horseback most of the day, mending fences as needed, collecting sheep, driving livestock. Daily, she helped bake yeast bread, cook beans and slabs of beef or legs of mutton, can, nurse the bum lambs, and watch her younger siblings. Midday, she carried jars of afternoon tea to the pasture. Somewhere in all of this, she completed her school lessons.

This was a land of not only hard work but also of hardship. Big brothers died of no one really knew what; premature twins set by the woodstove couldn't be saved. A grave couldn't be dug in the frozen ground. Until Spring, the babies lay in their handmade velvet-lined coffins in the far end of a shed. Living on a Montana ranch meant tough work and tough truths.

Marian valued her upbringing, but she wanted to go out on her own. She longed to travel; she dreamed of adventures. Her heart, she let her parents know, was set on nursing school. They struck a deal with her: if she would stay on an extra year and assume house duties and care for the three youngest children, her father would then take her to his sister in Chicago and help her enroll at Mt. Sinai. Marian's mother—who probably felt she'd earned a break—would go with her middle girls to board in town while they finished high school.

A year later, Mama tried to renegotiate the terms: one more year at home, she argued, and Marian could study to be a teacher. Dan Murphy, who normally surrendered to his wife's every whim, stood firm. "A promise," he said, "is a promise."

My mother-in-law never forgot that her father did the right thing by her, and she never forgot that her mother tried to do her wrong.

Despite her mother's objections, off Marian went to Chicago. She thrived. She studied and worked; she traveled. She brought brothers and sisters to be educated and paid their way. When war broke out, she signed on with the Navy and married an Army paratrooper. When they divorced, Marian packed up her son, Dan, and her daughter, Kathy. Back in Montana, she raised her children with an iron hand. They would do well in school, by God. They would be upright, and they would do as they were told. For the most part, they abided by her rules.

But one night, Dan slipped out of the house in the middle of the night to party with friends. Next morning, he woke to find his mother standing over the car he'd saved years to buy. She lifted the hood.

"I don't know much about what all this is," she said as she brought up her hammer. "But I am fairly certain I can do some damage." And if he hadn't shaped up, she most assuredly would have.

In the years before I knew Marian, she was becoming the person she was when we first met: a woman who cared not a whit for clothes or, actually, things in general. Her passions ran more toward travel and books, particularly Westerns, which she bought at yard or library sales. A dime, she thought, a fair price for a paperback. Wherever Marian went, Louis L'Amour went, too.

She liked Western movies as well, and movies about war. She liked her meat cooked to just this side of jerky. If you put the kettle on

31

and brought the water to a proper boil, she loved a cup of tea. She would sit at the table with a piece of toast and a home-canned peach and never need to utter a word. How different she was than we Southern women, with our compulsion to fill the very possibility of silence.

Like all the Westerners I've met over time, Marian appreciated a slice of pie, but she couldn't go without potatoes.

"If I don't get a potato every day," she told me as she ate a boiled one, "I feel like I haven't really eaten." That was the Black Irish in her.

And, oh, she loved a game of pinochle.

Dan and I were well into our second decade of marriage when we visited Montana for our niece's wedding. All the relatives who were currently speaking—those fiery tempers, you know—gathered for a night of cards. The numbers worked out, allowing everyone to participate at tables of four.

"But I don't know how to play," I admitted

"What!" a cousin exclaimed. "You're married to Dan Lovatt, and you can't play pinochle?"

"That's right," I said. "And what's more, I've never seen him play either."

This revelation dumbfounded the room.

Later I asked Dan privately, "What's up with the cards?"

"When it's thirty below for months on end, you spend all the time you can inside."

Things Marian didn't like: Jane Fonda topped the list—the mention of her name raised her blood pressure; "the city fathers," as she mockingly called local politicians; injustice. She also abhorred laziness and considered no job gender-specific. Everyone, she believed, should wash and fold and put away clothes. They should know how to iron and clean a house and change a tire.

Evidently, she'd had her fill of cooking before leaving for Chicago, so if her children wanted something other than frozen vegetables, stewed potatoes, and tough meat, they were encouraged to hone their skills in the kitchen as well. I have greatly benefitted from this philosophy. Dan braids our granddaughter's hair, sews on buttons, filets, sautés, and makes pickles. Bless you, dear Marian.

Another thing that boiled her blood: the mention of her mother. On no account should she be buried by Ma, she told her family. Stanley, the baby, could have that spot. Instead, her final resting place should be on the left side of her father.

Individually, and as a group, she told us, "I will not lie for eternity by someone who tried to go back on her word."

Those Irish, don't cross them. They know how to bear a grudge.

Although Marian never regretted much I know of, she did tell me she had been born a little too late. "I wished I could have been a pioneer," she lamented. "I would have been first in line on the wagon train."

"Really?" I asked. "A pioneer?"

"Oh, yes," she said dreamily. "I would have loved that."

Hmmm, I thought to myself. *She must not have seen those movies I grew up with—the ones where women were taken hostage or scalped, men burned alive, death by smallpox, cholera, typhoid. If you didn't die on the trail, you lived in a wagon.*

Me, I would have been one of those who turned tail and ran back East, but I didn't say so. By that time, I earnestly wished her to think me braver, better in every way, than I really was.

This Is the Day

April hath put a spirit of youth in everything.
William Shakespeare, "Sonnet XCVIII"

This Is the Day
Douglas Wyant

A neighbor's rooster crows.
Unseen birds warble.
I'm not a birder—
I can't identify birds by their calls,
except those that cry out their mournful names:
bobwhites and whippoorwills.

White clouds sail across the pale blue sky like ships under canvas.
Slender pine trees sway in a breeze like slow dancers.
All our flowering trees and shrubs are especially vibrant this spring.
Butterflies waggle their wings over the bountiful blossoms.
As I sit on the front porch in one of two weathered rocking chairs,
my mind flits from one idea to another like a bee gathering nectar.

This is the day the Lord has made....
Let everything that has breath praise the Lord.

Sources: Psalm 118:24 and Psalm 150:6.

Come On, Sweet Boy
Jayne Padgett Bowers

"The doctor's probably going to do a C-section," Carrie said, and I knew my daughter was walking that thin line between courage and fear. Seth was in the breech position, and although the doctor had turned him once, the stubborn little fellow soon eased his way back into what was comfy for him.

Sensing the apprehension in my oldest child's voice, I assured her that I would be there for the delivery. "Don't worry," I told her. "You still have a week until his due date, and a lot can happen by then."

Do all mothers spout off such optimistic words of comfort so easily? I wondered.

Despite the doctor's many assurances that everything was "just fine," I couldn't shake the edginess. This was my daughter's sixth child, and it had been nearly a decade since her perfectly formed, stillborn baby boy had briefly entered the family's life on a cold December night. Between then and now, there had been four live births.

The day of the scheduled section arrived, and my other daughter, Elizabeth, and I sped down I-95 on a sweltering July morning. Another scorcher! Neither of us what to expect or even how to think about the upcoming birth, so we rode mostly in silence, an unsettling sense of foreboding hovering between, above, and around us.

"Dad's coming, right?" Elizabeth asked.

"Said he'd be there. I sure hope so. Carrie needs all the support she can get."

"Mom, there's no use being so stressed out. It's not like my sis is an amateur at this. You're the one I'm worried about."

"Why? Just because I missed the first exit?"

"That...and the fact that you're driving so fast, nearly 80. Highway patrolmen are all over this stretch of highway."

"Okay, I'll try to calm down."

"I hope so," she said, restlessly rummaging through her bag. "You're making me nervous, too," Elizabeth said. "I can't even find my phone."

"Okay, okay. Want to stop at Cracker Barrel for a blueberry muffin or something?" I asked.

"Not really."

"Me either. I just want to get to Savannah and see your sister eyeball to eyeball."

Elizabeth put in her earbuds and closed her eyes, a sure indication that she wasn't in the mood for conversation. Neither was I. I tried listening to "This American Life" on NPR but soon gave up as my mind strayed to what the day held in store. Unbidden and unwanted, memories of my daughter's lost baby and his mother's grief flashed through my mind.

Arriving in steamy Savannah a couple of hours later, I maneuvered the Highlander into a skinny parking spot in the hospital's concrete parking garage, and Elizabeth and I darted to the entrance. After finally gaining admittance to the maternity ward, we hustled down the hall looking for Carrie. By now, she should be getting prepped for surgery, but where?

We soon found her room at the end of a long and brightly lit hallway. There she sat, propped against pillows, her husband Rich sitting in a chair to the left of the bed. Both looked anxious and preoccupied, fragile. *Be still my heart,* I told myself and forced a smile.

"Whew. Glad we got here before they took you to the OR. I'd have been upset if I'd missed you," I said, giving Carrie a fierce hug and then backing up for a good look at my daughter's troubled face.

"No danger of that," she replied with a wry frown, leaning in for a hug from her little sister.

"Why? Are they backed up in the operating room?"

"No, nothing like that. The doctor came in and tried one more time to turn the baby, and since he was able to without a problem, he thinks I should try a natural birth."

"So that's good, isn't it?" I asked, studying Carrie's expression.

"I guess so. It's good unless Seth decides to move again."

"We'll just have to trust the doctor."

"I know. I just wish they'd start the Pitocin."

Pitocin. From personal experience and study, I was all too aware of the strength of the labor-inducing drug. A synthetic form of oxytocin, it can quickly put a woman into what's been described as "hard-rocking" labor. I recalled its powerful and unrelenting effects when used to augment one of my own childbirth experiences and could hardly imagine what lay in store for my daughter who hadn't had a single contraction. *Zero to sixty* flashed through my mind.

Rich gently reminded her that it had only been a few minutes.

Again, "I know, I know."

Carrie had scarcely spoken when someone came in and whisked her away, our little entourage following close behind. Down halls, around corners, on an elevator, off an elevator, and down another hall, finally we arrived at the labor room.

Small, the room had a huge window on the far left side and a bed square in the middle of the tiled floor. Although the room was plain and utilitarian in look and feel, I sensed the magic of the drama that would soon unfold within its walls.

"So this is where we'll meet the newest family member, huh?" I asked no one in particular, my cheerfulness masking thoughts about the gravity of the baby's imminent passage from a warm, life-supporting environment to what could be a cold, frightening one. Though rare in the United States, some couples opt to ease the transition to life outside the womb by water birthing, a situation in which the mother gives birth in a pool of water.

Frankie, Carrie's father, arrived, bringing the number of adults waiting for Seth's appearance to four. Honing our small talk skills, we took turns sitting with the laboring mom, snacking in the hospital cafeteria, and strolling the halls. For hours, we waltzed in and out of the room, playing with Elizabeth's new iPhone, working crossword puzzles, watching TV, and waiting, waiting, waiting. More than once, I thought of Dumas' quote, "All human wisdom is summed up in two words, wait and hope."

Finally, the moment of birth approached, and the doctor shooed everyone out of the room except for Rich and a nurse.

Leaning over to give Carrie one last reassuring embrace, I said, "Gee, I hate to leave. I've never really seen a live birth, you know." I'd already expressed that regret three or four times throughout the day, and when no invitation was forthcoming, I reluctantly joined the others right outside of the room.

My former husband chuckled and said, "Did you really think that hint was going to help?"

"A grandmother can try, right?" I said, my head down, unable to meet his gaze. *Why couldn't they have relented just this once*, I wondered, aware of the increased tightness in my chest.

"You know how Carrie and Rich feel. They want it to be private, only the two of them and the doctor."

Just then, the door cracked open and Rich's head and shoulders appeared. "Hey Jayne, want to come inside?"

"You mean it?" I asked, overwhelmed with the realization of what I was about to witness. Frankie and Elizabeth stood staring at Rich, momentarily speechless at the summons.

Sweeping past Rich as he held the door ajar, I walked straight to Carrie and squeezed her hand, whispering "Thanks," before taking my position slightly behind the doctor and nurse.

The atmosphere in the room was electric, tense, serious. The nurse counted, and the doctor said, "Push." Many times. I hung back, glued against the far wall, wondering why I had felt so compelled to observe such an event.

"I see the head! One more push ought to do it," the doctor said.

Heart pounding, I inched forward to take a peek and gasped. I could see Seth's head, but something was wrong. His head was grayish-blue. *Where was his hair? Was that his brain barely covered by skin?*

His blue, limp body followed moments later. There was neither wail nor whimper.

The doctor called the NICU unit, and within seconds there were three additional nurses in the room. The atmosphere was charged with tension as they worked with the infant and the newfangled machines.

I turned away from Carrie towards the tiny lifeless form lying on the table. This was my grandson, and if medical personnel had even a modicum of confidence that he would breathe, so did I. Textbook after textbook affirmed the struggle of a baby making the transition from womb to world, some suggesting the elevation of heart rate as greater than anytime in a person's life except when having a heart attack.

Leaning over within inches of the table, I began whispering to him while one of the nurses cleared his airways, the sounds of suctioning filling an otherwise quiet room. As I watched, she cleaned the protective coating of vernix from his skin and massaged his tiny body. The other two nurses stood to my left, speaking to each other in muffled voices as they used the latest technology to monitor respiration and heart rate.

Crazy wild with panic, I tried to appear unruffled and calm. An onlooker might have interpreted my gentle tones as soothing, but I knew differently. There was suppressed alarm in my voice, and I wondered if the little one on the table could sense the urgency in my hushed utterances.

I was begging.

"Come on, Sweet Boy. Grandmama needs to see your pretty eyes." I glanced up at the nurse who nodded for me to continue. Leaning closer, I continued my entreaties, convinced that Seth would respond to the love and desperation emanating from my core.

"Time to open those eyes and join the world, Sweetie. Come on now."

From behind me, I heard my daughter's anxious voice. "Mama, what's wrong? I don't hear Seth crying. Is everything okay?"

"Everything's fine," I said, focusing on the baby lying before me, touching his tiny hand and waiting for the miracle I knew would come.

Never a child to back down easily, Carrie persisted in her questioning, her voice rising in panic.

"I want to see him," she demanded.

44

Helpless and unable to move from the bed, Carrie was dependent on the assurances of Rich and the doctor as the latter completed his ministrations.

"In just a minute. The nurse is getting him cleaned up."

Memories of a long ago December day flooded my mind as I continued to speak softly and imploringly to Seth. Although nearly a decade had passed, the loss of Carrie's first child was never far from my mind, and I did not, could not, see my daughter enduring such pain again. Beside her, Rich was murmuring words of comfort, and I focused all of my attention and energy on the newborn.

Stroking Seth's perfectly shaped head, I placed a hand on his motionless chest and silently prayed to the heavens above that I would feel the thump of a tiny heart.

I gulped before continuing in one steady, unbroken stream, "We've been waiting for you a long time, and Granddaddy, Aunt Libba, and I came all the way down here this morning just to see you. Wake up now. I want you to look at me when I tell you how precious you are, how lucky you are to be born to parents who love you so much."

As I continued to speak to Seth in the soothing tones used by women in all corners of the world when comforting a child, his skin gradually became rosy, and I remembered Annie Dillard's expression, "pinked up." My throat tightened as I watched the miracle unfold.

"Come on, Buddy. It's time."

I was down on his level, inches from his small face.

Seth opened his eyes and stared straight at me with a bright consciousness that seemed to ask, "Who are you?" We held the mutual gaze for several moments, communicating spirit to spirit, and when I looked up, the nurse gave me a teary-eyed smile and a thumbs-up.

I cried with joy and relief.

Suddenly aware of a muted conversation, I heard one of the nurses tell the doctor that all was well. "Seven," she replied to his query about Seth's APGAR score, a measurement system appraising the overall appearance and health of newborns. On a scale from 0 to 10, medical personnel rate infants on appearance, pulse, grimace, activity, and respiration. Amazingly, Seth's APGAR score at birth had been 1 and had quickly climbed to 7, then 8.

Seth Michael Maseda

My grandson was alive and well, his crying the best sound I'd heard all day, all year.

Awestruck by the wonder of birth and the fragility of life, I stood wordless and still beside him, a final moment between the two of us. Turning towards Carrie, I watched as a nurse gently placed Seth in his mother's waiting arms.

Sorry, Batman
Paddy Bell

My nephew, Brady, was making progress with the potty-training business and had advanced to cotton pull-up underwear. His were vividly festooned with super-hero images of Spiderman, Superman, the Ninjas, and others. One afternoon he sheepishly confessed to his mother that he'd had an accident.

"Oh, Brady. What is it you're supposed to say?" she asked in exasperation.

With absolute certainty came his humble-hearted response: "Sorry, Batman."

In my family, we tell and retell the Batman story and countless others as a way of remembering. The Baby Book, the official documentation of childhood transitions, just never seemed to gather steam with us. Once the willowy tufts of hair from first haircut, teeny kernels of lost teeth, and a few bits of construction paper artwork were archived, interest waned. Chronicling of consequential events and memorable incidents followed the well-intentioned road less traveled—deserted even.

Thankfully, we have kept the ancient tradition of oral storytelling alive. What follows are some precious and priceless moments from generations of children—moments that never made it into a baby book.

***

The same precocious Brady, during an assessment for nursery-school enrollment, had breezed through identification of all the shapes in question—the square, circle, and triangle.

"Very good, Brady. We're all done now," the tester smiled, patting him on the head.

"But what about the octagon?" Brady questioned. "Don't you have an octagon?"

This should not have been surprising, based on his older brother's recent evaluation for pre-Kindergarten. The standardized test identified base-line minimums for age-appropriate levels of performance. For example, at a certain age, children are expected to draw a stick person with essential elements of head, legs, feet, arms, hands, and possibly eyes and mouth. Four-year-old Cameron gripped the pencil tightly, his face hovering just inches above the paper, brow furrowed in deep concentration as he worked on his drawing.

After a few minutes, he looked up and announced, "Done!"

Most of the obligatory components were recognizable, and then some, including ears, spikes of hair, a carrot-like nose, and eyelashes. Exceptional added details were the tiny dots in the eyes for the pupils. But there was a problem—no hands. Eager to check the okay-box, the examiner took advantage of the one prompt allowed and said, "Look carefully, Cameron. If there's anything you want to add, you can do it now. Take your time to be sure."

Cameron scrutinized his stick person for a moment, then thumped the heel of his little hand on his forehead in that "Duh" gesture, rolled his eyes, and picked up the pencil. The tester must have felt deep relief, certain the mandatory hands were going to be attached.

Cameron turned the pencil point on its side and began to furiously scrawl over his entire illustration.

"There you go!" he announced, slamming his pencil down. "SKIN. I almost forgot the SKIN."

Notes and comments were written on the master sheet, but the okay-box wasn't checked. Still no hands. Pupils, eyelashes and skin are only extra credit if the basics are there. Government regulations!

***

Well-meaning adults often try to orchestrate situations to make unforgettable magical moments for children. Sometimes it backfires.

At the annual Christmas parade in 1955, thousands of parade-goers lined the streets in high anticipation of the arrival of Santa Claus. As in every year since anyone could remember, Santa's conveyance would be the town's pride and joy vintage fire truck, decked out in a profusion of boughs of cedar and pine, woven with red velvet streamers. The brass lanterns were polished to a blinding luster and adorned with bows and sprigs of holly.

On the popular corner of Washington and Columbus Avenues huddled a clump of adults who had colluded with Mr. Claus to make a personal greeting to my five-year-old cousin, Kathy. She stood mid-pack, being alternately hoisted by one or another adult for better visibility—for her to see St. Nick and for St. Nick to see her. Santa, a close friend of the family, was a willing conspirator to the plan. At the agreed-upon moment, he leaned over the side of the truck with a booming "Ho, Ho, Ho," and shouted, "Merry Christmas, Kathy! Merry Christmas!"

After a couple of bewildering blinks, Kathy gave an enthusiastic wave.

"Merry Christmas, Bob!" she shouted. "Merry Christmas!"

Oops.

***

It was a sunny spring morning, still holding a lingering winter chill in the air, as repairs were underway on the porch wooden railings. My four-year-old son, Ryan, and I settled on the porch swing to watch the progress. The child, intrigued with the hammer and nails and the leather tool belt wrapped around the handyman's waist, was also mesmerized by a relentless line of clear mucus running from the man's nose as he worked. For some time, a ratty bandana was retrieved to blow and wipe. But soon, a firm swipe of the jacket sleeve replaced the cloth. Ryan watched intently, captivated now by the rivulet as much as by the tools.

No doubt aggravated with the interruption of his work, the man finally decided to ignore the constant drip. But not Ryan.

He pointed to the stream of snot, and in a most helpful voice said, "It's down again, Mister."

***

"I wanna go with him," whined Mac to his grandmother.

"You're only five, too little to wander the streets. I've told you time and again."

"But I wanna…"

"No, Mac. Doc doesn't need a sidekick. He tears off through alleys and yards where little boys shouldn't go. You'll hear all about his adventures when he returns," she chuckled.

Mac did not want to hear yet again of Doc's exploits. This particular morning he decided to ignore his grandmother's warnings, and set off to join him, bolting out the back door to try to catch up.

Doc, a Collie-Dalmatian mix, lived up to his sagacious full name, Dr. Isaac Bickerstaff. This intelligent, clever, beloved charmer was quite the dog-about-town. When he wasn't off prowling, he gazed out the window of his Pleasant Street home, calculating the next opportunity for an airing. He didn't need permission. He'd just pop the door latch and make off on his rounds, which usually included a stop at the veterinarian office, where he was always welcome. Doc would take up station behind the reception desk, assume a sympathetic expression, and greet people and patients with his peculiar mouth noise—not a growl, not a bark, but a friendly crunching mew, like he had a mouthful of marbles.

Sometimes Doc sauntered out the Harrison Pike to the Boy Scout camp to swim with the campers in the river. Excessive rough-housing upset the dog, who couldn't always distinguish between play and evil intentions. If he sensed overzealous rowdiness, he would search for an opening, and get between the boys to break it up—gently, but with conviction.

Back in town, Doc knew to stop at Bianke's Restaurant where a bowl of blue-plate-special leftovers and a tin pail of cold water awaited him on the back steps.

Visions of the vet, the camp, Bianke's, enticing alleys and byways danced in Mac's little head as he ran to strike in with Doc for first-hand heroics.

The little boy didn't get further than a few houses down Pleasant Street before his grandmother collared him. All the way home she spanked his little bottom with a willow switch while he hollered, "Stop now, stop. That's enough!"

"I don't think it is enough, Mac."

"Oh yes, it is," he insisted, "Enough for now and ALL TIME!"

***

My brother, Danny, was three years old in 1956 when we were returning from Sunday church on a cold snowy Ohio winter morning. All were bundled up from head to toe, riding home in our 1952 Buick when Danny piped up, "Mommy, I have to go pee pee."

"Goodness, honey, we're almost home. Can you hold it?"

"I don't think so," he replied, squirming anxiously, "I've got my mittens on!"

***

Grandparents may assume too much, expect too much, convinced of the superior intelligence, talent, and aptitude of their grandchildren. When my granddaughter, Keensley, entered kindergarten, it seemed time to share the proud legacy of my membership in the Daughters of the American Revolution Society. I thought I was keeping it simple.

"Your great-great-great-great-great-great grandfather, Ebenezer Corey, fought in the battles of Lexington and Concord, among others. He fought to make America free."

"Oh, Grammy," Keensley asked with sparkling blue eyes full of hope and wonder, "Did he win?"

***

Keensley's younger brother, Griffin, skipped into the kitchen one morning with an eager greeting, "Hey, Dad, I really slept great last night."

"You sure did," my son told his three-year-old. "Good sleeping will make your muscles grow—make you strong. Let's see."

Griffin pushed up the sleeves of his blue Kentucky Wildcat pajamas, balled his fists, and flexed his arms to show his little biceps.

"Just as I thought," his smiling Dad said. "Stronger and taller, too. I'm pretty sure you grew some in the night."

The beaming child looked up, up, up at his six-foot, five-inch father and proudly stated, "Yep, Dad, you and I are about the same amount."

***

As the first grandchild born on both sides, as well as the first male born into the maternal side for three generations, my husband Rick was a special baby-boomer. On his second Christmas, the family decided that this holiday would be unforgettable with each and every adult relative playing their part for the toddler.

Presents filled the room, expanding far beyond the base of the luminous Christmas tree. Little Rick squealed at the sight, and dove in, helped and encouraged by family.

"Let's open this big package, Honey."

"Over here—look at the shiny red fire truck!"

"Open this one now, Ricky!"

On and on, the little boy worked through the morning as adults watched with delight, munched on gingerbread reindeer cookies and sticky buns, sipped eggnog in crystal punch cups, and nursed steaming coffee served up in the Christmas Spode china.

When the wrapping paper was gathered for throw-away, bows and ribbons carefully saved, and boxes stacked, all sat back with great satisfaction.

"A beautiful Christmas it was."

"Aren't these cowboy boots and little hat as cute as can be?"

"Did you see how high the fire truck ladder can be raised?"

"This fluffy teddy bear is *so* soft."

"Oh, yes, this was a perfect—a lovely Christmas."

They looked around, eyes twinkling, from tree to toys, to each other.

"Where's little Rick?"

"My goodness. Where *is* he?"

Sounds from the kitchen stirred them to action. Like a row of obedient ducklings, with great-grandmother in the lead, they waddled toward the noise. And there he sat. He had opened the cleaning cupboard and was joyfully playing with the vacuum attachments.

A lovely Christmas indeed.

***

These examples of golden verbal nuggets from children are deeply rooted in our family vernacular. "That's enough for all time," "It's down again, Mister," and "I've got my mittens on" have found countless applications through the years. As for teeth, hair, and Baby Book entries—well, "Sorry, Batman."

The Eleventh Commandment
LaShella Kirkland

There comes a time in every church-going child's life when we learn there are more than Ten Commandments. One through Ten may have been given to us by God, but the Eleventh is given to us by a power endowed by Him. And her name shall be known as Momma. And she said, "Thou shalt not cut up in church."

I learned this painful lesson in July 1972 as a five-year-old sitting on the fourth row pew of Rock Spring United Methodist Church. I was decked out in an itchy-owie dress: knee length, covered with frills, ribbons, and the hem decorated with dime-sized pink flowers and scratchy lace around the collar. Underneath, I wore white bloomers layered with three rows of frills and little pink-lace ankle socks. And, being a proper lady, I even wore lace gloves, a matching hat, and a little purse. Momma styled my hair into two ponytails which fell below my shoulders, both ends tied with pink satin bows.

I'm not sure what was going on in my mind that particular Sunday—maybe the heat coupled with all of that lace. Or as my Grandma Mary used to say, "Child, the devil must have gotten into you." Who knows? Boredom, I guess. So I decided to have a little fun and play the mockingbird game.

Reverend Fried Chicken was whopping and hollering in the pulpit. My parents gave him that nickname because the first thing he did after service every Sunday was peck around for somebody's house he could impose himself on for a free dinner. I guess he really liked fried chicken. Well, that day, I decided to mock him. Every time he screamed, "Jesus! Glory! Hallyluya! Can I get an Amen?" I did the same.

"Glory, ham mercy, Lawd!"

But that wasn't enough for me. I needed to make it stick. So I jumped up from my seat, fell into the aisle, rolled around on the red carpet like the grown folks did when they got "happy." Fried Chicken stopped and just stared at me being touched by the Spirit. I was touched alright, but not by the Holy Spirit. This Spirit yanked me by my left arm and lifted me off the floor.

"Get yo' butt back in that seat! Have you lost your ever-loving mind?" Momma hissed. I looked up at her with a straight face.

"NO!" I yelled as loud as I could.

A dead silence fell over the entire congregation. No one moved. They all sat there like they had just seen a haint. I didn't get scared until I looked at Momma's face. Something flashed across her eyes like lightning, and for a moment I thought I saw two horns on top of her head.

Then verily, verily, calmly and sweetly, she said, "Let's go to the car. I've got some candy for you."

"Yippee. Okay."

She took my left arm and led me out of the church. The usher opened the doors for us. As he was closing them, he gave me this pitiful look like I was in trouble. We walked to our dark green 1968 Ford—my daddy's pride and joy. It had a white top, pea-green seat, and an AM radio. When we got to the passenger's side door, Momma told me to stand still while she got the candy. She opened the door, reached under the seat and pulled out her thick, black leather belt.

Uh-oh.

She *to'e* my little red butt up. The *whupping* may have lasted for a few minutes but in kid time, it felt like hours. My beautiful pink dress was outshined by my tear-stained red face. And all the while, she kept yelling, "Don't you ever show out like that again! Stop all that crying *'fore* I give you something else to cry for!"

LaShella at Six

You mean to tell me there's something else?

She took a break to catch her breath. Lawd knows I needed to catch mine. The next part of the whupping resembled a dance routine. The only difference, she knew all of my moves better than me. If I twirled around clockwise, the belt would meet me counterclockwise. Two steps to the left then snapped three to the right.

Then I was paraded inside.

58

I had to walk back into that church and face all those people staring at me. We went back to our seats and sat down. I wouldn't look at anyone. How could I? Everybody *knew* what had happened. They *knew and approved*. I felt betrayed. Not one person had enough decency to give me a handkerchief, a hug, or a smile. The only thing I got was the *uh-huh* look. Traitors. They were all on her side. I did the only thing I could do. I lay down on the seat and went to sleep.

Ten years later, my baby brother Jean would learn the same lesson when he turned five. He didn't learn it like I did on a Sunday. He learned it on a Wednesday night in June during revival. Jean was Momma's precious baby—a boy so bad that one day I decided to check his scalp for the numbers 666. Convinced that she had given birth to the Antichrist, I wanted to fulfill my sworn Christian duty to rid the world of this demon. I never found any numbers, but on that Wednesday night, Momma's baby was truly possessed.

She was singing up on the choir platform. Jean and I sat in the audience near the doors. All of a sudden, he jumped up from his seat and started running around in the church whooping and hollering. When he stopped, he reached behind the seats and threw a bunch of hymnals on the floor. Then he fell down and continued screaming. I couldn't believe my eyes. *This child is crazy.* I knew Momma would take care of this, but for some reason, I decided to intervene and save him. I ran over and ordered him to sit down.

He politely told me, "I don't have to listen to you. *You* go sit down!"

Dear Lawd, please ham mercy on his little butt.

Momma verily, verily, calmly and sweetly, stepped down from the choir platform and walked over to him. A job had to be done. She whispered something in his right ear. Everyone had the *uh-huh* look on their faces. She snatched baby boy up by his left arm and marched him towards the doors.

But right as they passed me, Momma's brat stuck out his forked-tongue at me.

"Ha-ha," he said. "I'm going to get some candy and you ain't going to get none."

Ten minutes later the doors opened and Jean's march of shame began: flushed face, sniffling, a handprint on his left cheek, and the *uh-huh* looks from everyone. She deposited him on the seat right in front of me. I just had to ask.

"Did you get your candy?"

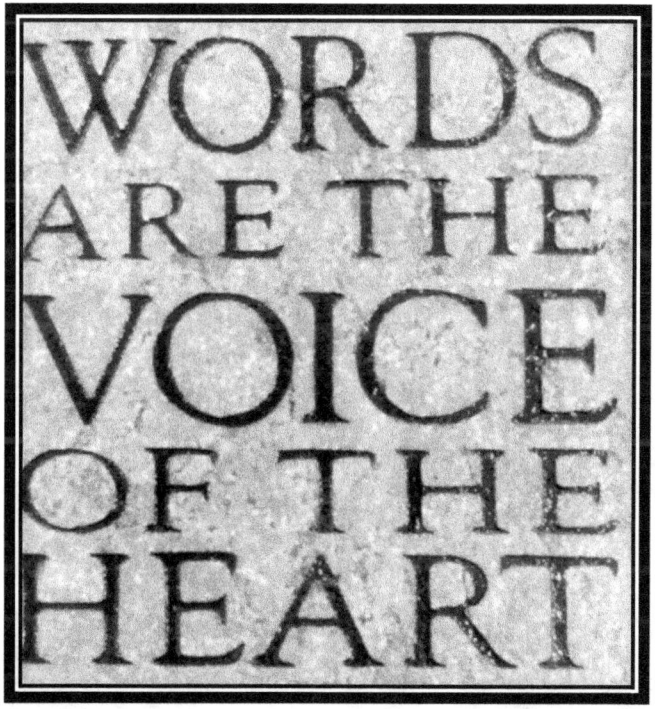

Introduction to Jasmine Rhythms
Paddy Bell

Jasmine Rhythms is the result of my creative collaboration with composer Dick Goodwin. This work was commissioned by the Columbia Choral Society and had its inaugural performance May 20, 2016, in Columbia and May 22, 2016, in Camden. The entire piece is

composed of seven movements; four are included in this anthology.

In 1924, South Carolina legislators voted to adopt the yellow jessamine, Latin translation, jasmine evergreen, as the state flower. The more I researched, the more obvious it became that this little blossom's intriguing characteristics parallel our own in many ways and reflect the human spirit. It lives hard, wild, fast and free, packing many adventures in its short life span as it struggles to achieve great heights. The four movements included here represent the jasmine's appearance at the end of winter, "Winter Showdown," the carefree and wild growth of the jasmine vine in every corner of the state, "Vagabond Gypsy," a tribute to some of South Carolina's other state symbols, "Jasmine Time," and the flower's yearning for a much deserved restful sleep, "Come, Holy Hour."

Perseverance, hope, despair, love and loss, and ultimately life and death are themes that Dick and I celebrated with every word and musical note, so that this work will resonate on levels far beyond the simple life cycle of a plant. All writers hope their words are read— simply read. Having them evolve into a masterful piece of music was beyond my wildest imaginings, and such an honor.

Jasmine Time
Lyrics, Paddy Bell

The earth maneuvers slightly, leaning closer to the sun,
romantic wistful fancies seem to occupy the young,
polliwogs turn into frogs, scuppernongs get riper,
Carolina Wren again join the woodland choir.

Spotted salamander slink to shallow ponds to breed,
pin-striped bass meander, caring not to sprint nor speed,
ladybugs in polka-dots end their hibernation,
hightail to the backdoor screen, resume their conversation.

Spaniels sleep on porches, dream of days retrieving geese,
sweetgrass bow and curtsy at the bidding of a breeze,
smoky clouds of mayflies cruise indigo-tinted skies,
springtime endeavors to untether time and tides.

Then the polecat and the possum shag in the meadow,
pines and the palmetto sway in syncopated time,
the crescent moon is waxing, old folk are relaxing,
buds begin to blossom, Jasmine start to climb.

Jasmine time, Jasmine time.

Washday
Myra Yeatts

Aunt Minnie, a widow who had come to stay with us motherless children, took a prideful pleasure in her wash. "You can be poor," she would say, "but there's no excuse for being dirty." Her sheets, and everything else that was white, went into the big iron pot. Boiling the whites with lye soap was her mark of distinction. White took on a whole new meaning on washday.

My sister and I, on the other hand, hated washday. I didn't want to lose my neighborhood troop of playmates who helped me act out the Western from the previous Saturday afternoon picture show. We had a tendency to kick up a lot of dust from our clean-swept yard while playing cowboys and Indians.

Janice, ten years my senior, despised the unending work of washday. She and my brother, Jay, always hung the laundry. As it dried, she was expected to iron everything: shirts, pants, dresses, sheets, even underwear. Aunt Minnie had a theory that clothes lasted longer if they were ironed.

Janice had thrown a tantrum that morning. She and her friends had planned to go to the lake for a picnic. At sixteen, she was allowed to date for the first time, but an all day trip, on washday, was out of the question.

As I kept my vigil in the washhouse, I could still hear my sister's tirade. "Myra doesn't do anything around here. I have to work from sunup to sundown. It's not fair."

Even my fourteen-year-old brother, Jay, got into the act. "Yeah, and the poor little sickly thing drinks all the milk. I had to drink water for breakfast this morning."

Aunt Minnie quickly came to my defense, "She's the baby, and she's still getting over her sore throat. Now you all just go on and get them clothes hung out. Work first, play later," she said as she carried another laundry basket out the back door.

I looked up to find two pairs of unfriendly eyes staring at me. "I didn't do anything," I whined.

"Of course not, you're the baby. You *are* just the cutest little thing. You're just little Miss Perfect, and you better get your little perfect self out of my sight, if you know what's good for you. Go!"

I backed away from their anger and stumbled down the steps to find the protection of Aunt Minnie. But the blistering words still reached me.

"You're a little actress, is what you are. You might fool Aunt Minnie, but we know better. You're just a little brat," said Janice.

I felt lower than a snake's belly. I thought my sister to be the most beautiful girl in the world, and my brother was so smart he could make fire with two sticks. Unfortunately, most of the time, they didn't like me.

I went to the washhouse and watched Aunt Minnie pick up the

white shirts out of the boiling water with an old broken plow handle and toss them into the wringer washer. I'd seen it a hundred times. I sighed with boredom, pulled my marbles out of my pocket, and squatted on the dirt floor to practice shooting. The fire crackled and spit under the wash pot and Aunt Minnie made me move further away.

Looking out the door from my new location, I saw my siblings giggling at the clothesline. Something was up, but better not to ask. They'd just run me off or lock me in the chicken coop. Better to keep my distance for a while. I stayed put when Aunt Minnie went back in the house.

Janice was probably ironing because the radio played, and I could hear Doris Day singing, *"Que sera, sera, whatever will be, will be."*

I got up and peeked out the door and saw the reason for my siblings' mirth. A moment later, the screen door slammed and Aunt Minnie appeared. At the same time, a shiny new Buick pulled into our driveway. The driver, a deacon from the church, became mesmerized by the clothesline.

There, facing the driveway and the road into town, on the front clothesline, framed by the startlingly white sheet behind them, hung Aunt Minnie's new pink nylon bloomers. They were stretched to their fullest capacity and seemed to cover half the sheet.

My breath caught in my throat, and I hid behind the door. Peeking through a knothole in the washhouse wall, I watched as Aunt Minnie stopped on the back stoop and looked proudly at the full lines of clean clothes. She looked once, then twice, her hand slowly coming up to her mouth.

Mr. Frank got out of his car and tried unsuccessfully to avert his eyes from the offending garment. His jaw hung loosely. He blinked several times and wet his dry lips before he could meet Aunt Minnie's frozen face.

Time stood still. Through the screen door, my sister's horrified face took it all in. Her mouth formed a large O.

Then, as if nothing had occurred, Aunt Minnie and Mr. Frank began to congenially discuss the upcoming Primitive Baptist Church Association meeting. Mr. Frank led Aunt Minnie toward his new car as he prepared to leave. He said, "It's my turn to take unleavened bread for communion to this meeting, and I was wondering, since I'm a widower and all, maybe I could get you to make it for me. I'd be mighty grateful to you and would be happy to pick you up and take you...and the bread to church Sunday."

I heard no more but took that opportunity to make a dash for the house and away from that pink picture. I found my sister in tears, ironing furiously and conceding that she would never be allowed to get out of the house for the rest of her life. "But that won't be long," she said, "because she's going to kill me." She glared at me nastily through her tears and said, "Of course, if you had done it, it would be just fine. Go on, get out of here, and stop staring at me!"

Retreating to the door, I saw Aunt Minnie approach the house, head down and in a hurry. I looked back over my shoulder at my soon-to-be executed sister and took a deep breath.

Blocking the doorway as I grinned broadly, showing where my two front teeth should be, I announced, "I'm a good helper. I'm tall enough to hang out clothes now. I hung up your pretty new underwear for you."

My acting debut may not have been the most believable performance, but as it turned out, Aunt Minnie seemed distracted and a little flushed. I don't think she cared who hung up her underwear. She swept me up in her arms and gave me a big hug before returning to the washhouse.

Janice looked at me with disbelief. Slowly, a big smile broke on her face, showing that pretty dimple. Behind her, Jay snorted with laughter.

That washday became a pivotal point in our family. My siblings and I grew closer as Aunt Minnie spent more and more time with Mr. Frank and away from our home.

A Bushel and a Peck
Kathryn Etters Lovatt

Before real summer sets in, something very much like a peach comes to market. Leathery skin wraps around leathery innards, the flesh of the fruit clings whole-heartedly to its pit. These early pickings are scrawny, tragically devoid of scent, and perfectly irresistible. My father used to scorn them. "Bah," he'd proclaim, "a May peach," although the next month would be well upon us. We ate them anyway, him complaining and me resigned. A May peach, or a June one for that matter, is better than no peach at all.

Later, in the height of full harvest, we'd stand side-by-side and devour dead-ripe Redhavens over the huge double sink of my parents' kitchen. There, in those months, in those moments of immeasurable abundance, the true and imagined stories of my young life still play out. In the background, tractors drone like a soundtrack. Outside, it's dripping hot.

In the baby-booming deep South of the Fifties, summers felt as if the blazing fist of Vulcan, Roman god of fire, punched through the sky and landed a blow in the middle of South Carolina. Temperatures rose to the danger zone as school let out for the year. The thermometer refused to back down until after Labor Day, longstanding signal for classes to start again. The stinging heat drove up vines, bolted stalks and would, in due time, turn tomatoes brilliant red. Garden patches tendered okra, peppers, melons, corn, far too many squash and every kind of bean ever cultivated.

Although lone air-conditioners teeter-tottered in windows of privilege, most everyone else took shelter on porches or under shade trees. Church fans and fly swatters were held in high regard. Even early mornings swarmed with pesky things that stung or bit or, scarier still, ones that might strike. My big brother happily ran amok in the fields and swamps, but I was too young to go my own way. A few weeks into summer vacation, a muggy boredom

My mother, my brother and me

began settling over the early afternoons. Not even our dogs showed interest in play. They dug holes and hunkered down in the cool dirty-dirt below the white sands from the beginning of time. A sharp twig to the homes of doodlebugs and an ominous refrain failed to persuade a one to surface. Ants had laid claim to the climbable mimosa.

My mother carried the daily weight of me looking for something to do as long as she could. That took us roughly through lunch. "All right," she'd say as she put away the final plate. Momma put me in the car and drove nearly fifteen miles to her mother's. Grandma did not suffer whiners.

We entered by a side door straight into the kitchen, a room we hardly ever left while inside. Rather than the aroma of baking cookies, the savory smell of streak-of-lean, cousin-once-removed to poor fatback, filled my grandmother's house. This esteemed all-purpose seasoning of old Southern cooks could have been detected even if nothing bubbled on the stove eye or roasted in the oven—although I recall no such occasion.

If Grandma wasn't baking, she was canning; she blanched, pickled or jellied whatever ripened. She gloried in what looked like drudgery, particularly for a woman her size, a powerhouse of a redhead who came from days when mills worked children of twelve, her among them. Perhaps that early hard labor set in motion the belief that no one, on any account, should sit idle.

Oblivious to the heat rising in vapors from her stove, she would, for our sakes, fling open the back and front doors and send me to flip the switch to her attic fan. A cyclone ensued. Any piece of loose paper lifted, lolled and scattered. Selma, the wide-bottomed calico cat, twitched her tail at whatever happened to fly by. That stiff wind carried no power to cool by day, only the draw of the soft night air could do that, but pointing out the fan's failings might be interpreted as a complaint. If griping was a symptom of sloth, work was its tonic, and Grandma never fell short of chores even a little girl might do: drying silverware, filling a wheelbarrow with pinecones, dusting. The one task I never minded started with the lowly bean.

A man with a truckload of vegetables pulled regularly into the road by my grandmother's house. He came early mornings, first to her—or so he said and so she believed—to let her take the pick of his produce. On those days, my mother and I would arrive and find a pitcher of grape Kool-Aid, iced and waiting. Grandma went straight to her thickly draped dining room, and out she would come with a split-wood basket, tall and conical, brimming beyond its bushel walls with something so fresh, bugs thrived on the outside and gorged themselves with what lay within. Her very favorite something was beans, better still if they were butterbeans, and best of all, speckled butterbeans. Not simply colored, mind you.

No matter what the sciences assert, I have it on good authority that there is indeed a difference. Raw speckled beans, my sources declare, glisten like semi-precious stones. They brandish the purples of amethyst, from pale lavender to veins shocked with port wine. They

shine like opals, translucent gems traced with fire. From experience, I know this to be true, and I know that before their full array can be properly admired, a veritable heap of them must be shelled.

Our shelling took place on the front porch. My mother and I always sat on the green glider, an enamel pan between us. My grandmother, in one of two matching rockers, always expected her younger daughter any minute. My aunt—she of weak wrist and a Friday standing appointment with Audrey, queen bee of hair-dos and manicures in our small realm—usually showed up. We were begrudgingly glad to see her.

Mae pulled her chair from our circle, outside the breeze of the Emerson table fan, black and heavy as cast iron. Powered by a frazzled tail of a cord, the blades turned like dervishes, high being the one and only speed, and the force certainly would have mussed my aunt's French twist. Her distance from the three of us also separated Mae from the tower of beans and the communal aluminum catchall for spent shells. She used most of her energy going up and down to dispose of an empty pod or two and adding her meager garner to Grandma's pool of beans. Never mind, we were together, as important to our rhythm as the task before us.

A butterbean is like an oyster. The sides hold together in a clamp and the knife that opens the coupling is your thumbnail. This single gesture should split the shell wide open and the beans spill out with the slightest nudge. Simple enough. But the juices and the repeated motion offend the tender quick beneath the nail and rub the surrounding skin raw. And yet, we gathered eagerly. The others' mouths might have watered at the prospect of speckled beans with a side of biscuit, but I wasn't there for the beans. I was there for the talk.

This was our campfire, a solitary time and place to tell tales. Grandma did most of the telling. Sometimes she began with healers and dreamers of dreams, stories from the Bible, but in short order she fell back into the unfathomable mire of horror. Edgar Allan Poe had nothing on her. Time and again, she scared me speechless with body parts in cellars, whispers in the night, a dead woman tapping at the window. I can only suppose my mother allowed me to hear about people being buried alive because she wanted to hear about people being buried alive. In any case, these anecdotes could be depended upon to quicken the pace of our shelling.

Her best story, a ghost story she vowed to be true, was told in first person. It took place, naturally, one dark and stormy night. A crack of lightning and a pounding on the door roused her. She didn't nudge my grandfather awake—she wasn't that kind of a woman—but got up out of bed and went to the door. There, drenching wet, stood Uncle Hazard, kin from my grandfather's side, kin who lived an entire state away. He shook himself off as she unlatched the screen.

"What in the world are you doing here?" Grandmother asked as she ushered him in. He'd paid a visit to his son in Columbia he told her and thought he would stop by and say hello. "Let me go tell Tyrie," she said, referring to my grandfather, Tyra. But by the time Granddaddy pulled on his pants, threw on a shirt and got to the living room, no one was there.

"He was standing in this very spot."

Grandmother pointed to a damp ring by the door.

"What on earth made him go?"

My grandparents decided to telephone in the morning. Call long distance, not an everyday event. Or someone called them. Or maybe it was one way one time, and another the next. I didn't care. Still don't, because to this day, the story gives me a satisfying chill. And you know what? Of course, you do. Uncle Hazard had died in his bed that same night.

This was not a story my grandmother told every time we shelled beans, but it was definitely a bean story, and one she could almost always be persuaded to tell if they were speckled.

To everyone's surprise, my grandmother was mere flesh and blood. She left without coming to anybody's door.

From the memory of watching, my mother cooked the foods of her mother's life and of her own. She searched each summer for beans. One year, she heard about a shelling machine and she wanted to take a look. I drove thirty miles down roads only my father and the family who lived at the dusty end must have been able to find with ease. A man brought out a big plastic bag. Mother held the bag up and handed the bag back. We left without a single bean. Technology had a ways to go before it could mechanically shell and leave the beans intact.

A few years later, a place named Lee's Peas and Beans opened up. Theirs were shelled, but whole and firm. They had some speckled ones, or maybe they were only colored. We bought a bushel. The woman who sold them to us turned to me.

"Do you blanch your beans?" she asked. I looked at Mother. She nodded.

"We do," I said.

The woman, deferring again to my mother's age and careful perhaps not to question experience, delivered her advice to me instead.

"If you take them home and wash the field dust off real good and just put them in a bag and cover them with water, I think you'll be satisfied."

My mother had to speak up then. "Don't blanch them?"

"No ma'am."

"Hrumph," my mother said in the car. "I'll try one quart."

She pulled her test bag of beans from the freezer not long after and cooked them as usual. They tasted like they came fresh from the garden. She shook her head. "I'll be," was all she had to say.

After that, we looked for Lee's truck or drove to the farm, but once or twice a season, Momma would find a mess of beans in the store or by the road and buy them both for old time's sake and because a bean out of the shell and into the pot is like a trout from the brook to the pan.

We would sit at the table, my mother, father and me, and later my daughter Brie would take a chair. Sometimes, oh, nearly every time, I would say, "Remember that awful story Grandma had about Uncle Hazard?" But Momma would act like she couldn't quite, so I would have to tell every detail and a few of my own. As we sat there popping open shells and tossing the contents into the bowl my mother inherited, I realized the beans were never as purple as in my imagination. Still, they made a sweet little sound as they hit the enamel. *Plink, plink-plonk*, they sang, every bean adding to the pile, every note adding to the tune.

The Friendship Risk
Mindy Blakely

I wasn't normally the type of person to go out on a limb. I approached others with caution or shyness on first meeting them and didn't normally open up until I knew them better. I longed to find a friend I could really trust. After spending three weeks at Winthrop College in Rock Hill, South Carolina, I had met a large number of classmates, but I still felt alienated and alone. Where should I look for someone who wouldn't laugh at my ideas, who would be supportive and dependable, and who would keep my secrets safe? I never imagined I'd find the answer on a trip to the movies.

Dana and I headed out around 6:30 to catch the 7 p.m. feature, *Risky Business*, at the small movie theatre a few blocks from school. As we walked closely past the gurgling fountain in front of Tillman Hall, the administration building, a burst of water sprinkled us, but it felt refreshing in the nearly 70 degree temperature. Birds chirped in nearby trees as we strolled beside the freshly mowed green grass toward Oakland Avenue.

"Mindy, have you seen it yet?" Dana asked.

"Seen what?"

"The ghost."

"What ghost?" I brushed my long brown hair over my right shoulder.

"The ghost that haunts our residence hall," she said.

We lived in the oldest dormitory, Margaret Nance Hall, originally built in 1895. The L-shaped building in the center of the campus contained three floors and housed approximately 250 students. Originally called North Dormitory, the hall was renamed in 1925 to honor Margaret White Johnson Nance, mother of founding president David Bancroft Johnson.

"During World War I," Dana continued, "a student was expelled because she got pregnant. That same day, she received a letter informing her that her boyfriend had been killed in France. Legend says she hung herself. Some students say they've seen her standing at the top of the staircase late at night."

"Oh, no. Don't tell me that."

Our building had no elevator, and my room was on the third floor at the top of those stairs. I couldn't handle an encounter with a spirit. I could barely communicate with humans.

"Ghosts aren't real, Silly," Dana said.

"I know, but now I'll be creeped out every time I climb those stairs late at night."

"Sorry," she giggled.

***

Dana and I had met through a mutual friend, but we hadn't spent much time together yet. I knew she'd grown up in the small town

81

of Harleyville, near Charleston. She informed me that the town was not populated with motorcycle fanatics, and she didn't own a motorcycle herself.

I also knew that she'd played on her high school basketball team. She stood about five-foot-eight, I guess, compared to my five-foot-four height. So, in an effort to generate small talk, I asked about her basketball experience.

"Oh, I have a great idea," she said. "We should totally go to the men's basketball game tomorrow night."

Yikes! That conversation starter backfired.

Winthrop didn't have a football team. The big sports draw had become men's basketball. I didn't want to hurt her feelings, but I hated both football and basketball.

"Well," I said, "I'm not really a huge basketball fan."

"That's because you've never been to a game with me. Since I used to play, I can teach you all the lingo and explain everything that's happening. We're gonna have so much fun. I can't wait."

I watched squirrels chasing each other from tree to tree and resigned myself to enduring a boring basketball game as a necessary sacrifice in the search for a pal. We walked in silence for a while, and I struggled to think of something witty to say.

A male student passed us carrying a female student piggyback style on his shoulders. Suddenly, Dana leaped backwards out of the path of a flying neon green Frisbee. "What do you like to do for fun?" she asked.

"I love to read novels," I said, "and I fancy

myself a writer of poetry and short stories."

"That's so cool. I couldn't write anything to save my life, and I hate to read unless I'm trying to fall asleep." She laughed, absently running a hand through her short black hair.

"My writing isn't very good," I admitted, "but it helps me relax."

"I'd love to read something you've written sometime."

"We'll see." I wasn't yet sure I trusted her, or anyone else, to read my writing.

We didn't appear to have much in common, but I was enjoying the conversation, and at least the movie would provide a distraction. We meandered down the street past the Delta Delta Delta sorority house and the Sigma Alpha Epsilon fraternity house.

"How do you like college so far?" Dana asked.

I picked a piece of lint from my blue jeans. "I've met a lot of people, but it's different than I thought it would be."

"I know what you mean. It seems like all anybody wants to do is drink."

"Right!" I kicked a rock out of my path. "And I couldn't spend another evening watching other students playing quarters. Talk about boring."

"What game is that?"

"You know, the one where someone flips a quarter into a plastic cup of beer. If they succeed, they drink the beer. If they lose, their opponent drinks the beer. Either way, the game doesn't end until everyone is too wasted to play anymore."

"Oh, that game." She stopped to tie her tennis shoe. "I don't want to judge anyone else, but I grew up in a Christian home. I don't drink."

"Really? Same here. My family is Southern Baptist, and I don't drink either. I usually just watch everyone else and feel idiotic. I went out with an old buddy last night, and I couldn't even finish one beer. The vile taste alone nearly made me want to puke. Thanks so much for inviting me to a normal non-alcoholic activity. I desperately needed a change."

We both laughed then grew quiet. We passed Winthrop Lodge, a former motel now converted to off-campus student housing. The seedy looking place with a crumbling orange roof and white stucco walls supposedly hosted many wild parties and drug deals. We hastened our pace to a near run.

"Hey, want to join me and my roommate when we go to O'Sullivans next Thursday?"

Had I heard her correctly? O'Sullivans was an upscale nightclub on the other side of town. "I thought you said you didn't drink."

"I don't, but I really, really love to dance, so I usually just tag along and order a Coca-Cola."

"They'll let you order a Coke at a nightclub?"

"Yeah, they have to have Coca-Cola to make rum and Cokes."

"But will they serve you just a Coke without rum or anything else in it?"

"Of course. That way, we don't have to consume alcohol, but we can still hang out with the college crowd. All the cute guys from our classes will be there."

"Count me in then," I said. "I love to dance, too, and you better believe I want to be where the cute guys are."

We giggled. My sneakers crunched over the gravel parking lot of the theatre.

"Speaking of good looking boys, have you met anyone interesting yet?" Dana asked.

"Oh, girl, yes. My acting class elective is full of possibilities. I'm convinced one fellow really is Walter from the Bi-Lo advertisements. Another guy makes me laugh every time I see him. He stands about six feet tall with curly orange-red hair. I think he looks just like Ronald McDonald. I also met a handsome lad with curly dark hair, brown eyes, and the most fun personality ever, but guess what?"

"He's gay!" We shout in unison and laugh.

"Why are the cute ones always gay?" Dana asked.

"I don't know. I can't understand it, because I'd totally date him."

We bought refreshments and took our seats in the middle of the darkened theatre. I popped some Goobers in my mouth and slurped from the Pepsi in my cup holder. We got lost in the story. The film challenged me to be daring and let my guard down.

As soon as we returned to the dorm, I kicked off my shoes and performed my imitation of the famous Tom Cruise sock slide across our wooden floor. Dana immediately followed me. Laughter erupted as we sailed down the halls, nearly colliding with other students.

We stayed up another hour, laughing and talking and reciting our favorite lines from the flick. When I finally closed my door, I couldn't wipe the smile from my face.

A Million Little Worlds

We are an impossibility in an impossible universe.
Ray Bradbury

Summer

Megan Bevan

Dog-chased grasshoppers leap to brittle stalks of wheat
carried by wisps of wind and veined wings.
Pastured animals bask in tepid waves of sunbeam
or cool beneath elms in fields banked by farmers' ponds
where trout gorge on fat flies
and grandchildren sort trapped tadpoles
and wade barefoot,
letting red mud mingle between toes
and dry to stained crusts.

Another Side of the Family
Myra Yeatts

I inched my small frame tightly against the hallway wall and closer to the porch where the women sat after Sunday dinner. I meant to find out what was going on. Earlier, their gossiping and excited laughter dried up when I walked into the kitchen.

Aunt Minnie, Daddy's sister and my caretaker for as long as I could remember, sat on the porch surrounded by her sisters. The men stood around or leaned on parked cars in the driveway and yard with their hat brims pulled down to give a little protection from the August sun. They smoked cigarettes or dipped snuff while they listened to the Cardinals baseball game on the car radio.

"What does Jappie think about all this?" asked Aunt Cora. She was a sister-in-law and mighty nosey.

"He don't say much. You know that. I reckon he's like the rest of us. Worried about Myra," said Aunt Minnie. "He wants his young'un to be all right."

"Minnie, you know good and well that Mama intends to stay on," said Mavis, her sister. "She'll take good care of Myra."

"I don't know what's best," said Aunt Minnie.

I peeked out the front door and watched her start to wring her hands and knew she was getting all worked up. She didn't like being pestered.

But Mavis kept on talking, "I think that's why Mama decided to spend the weekend with Herman. Even if he is her favorite son, she don't like living there much. I'm pretty sure she's packing up everything at Herman's to move here."

Aunt Minnie pushed away from the women and stood on the edge of the porch with her back to them. Her voice cracked when she said, "Seems like she ought to talk to Jappie about that first, wouldn't you think?"

Aunt Mavis went and stood beside her and patted her back. "You don't need to be worrying about such. You need to be thinking about what you will be wearing on your wedding day."

The other women began to cackle. "And what you'll be wearing on your wedding night," said Aunt Cora.

The hair on the back of my neck stood up, and the fried chicken I had eaten for dinner rose up in my throat.

Aunt Minnie was getting married. She had been with me since my mother died when I was two years old. Nine years. The past couple of years felt different because she'd been going on dates with Mr. Frank. Both my brother and my sister had left during that time too. Janice worked at a bank in Norfolk, and Jay had joined the Navy. Grannie lived with us most of the time now. Too old to live alone, she was supposed to visit each of her children on a rotating basis. But it seemed like she preferred our house.

Now she might stay forever.

She didn't like me. I was willful. She said I acted like the tenant farmer trash my mother had come from. I couldn't count the times she would remind me of her side of the family with the plantation and the big cotton and tobacco crops. "Remember who you are." She told me "Everything you do wrong, God writes it down in a book with your name on it. When it gets full, He gives it to the devil and you'll burn for eternity."

I spent my days dreaming instead of studying. She'd say, "Why can't you be like your cousins? They stay on the honor roll all the time. All you want to do is read and watch the picture show every Saturday."

I did my best to corrupt my cousins when they came to visit. I made up stories, loosely borrowed

Grannie

from the Kenly Movie Theater Westerns. But in the last year, my girl cousins had drifted away. "I don't want to get my dress dirty. Why don't you sit on the porch with us and talk?" asked my pretty cousin, Linda, who was not quite a year older than me. I just looked at her and wondered if getting boobs made her sick. Then I ran off with the boys, playing tag through the corn rows of the garden.

At age eleven, I could outrun all my male cousins and led them in our adventures. We played games fearlessly in the graveyard which bordered our property. And I scared them as often as possible with stories of ghosts and noises in the night. They liked coming to my house because I had a good imagination.

But my imagination sometimes proved not to be my friend. As I leaned against the wall of the long hall, I looked at the closed doors of the bedrooms. Everyone left me. The empty rooms filled with ghosts. Sometimes my married sister, Ruby, visited with her babies, but mostly the house creaked and groaned with the memories of the fun and laughter that no longer lived in those rooms. Just me and Daddy. I swallowed hard.

Daddy and I had an understanding. He would tell me stories and read to me. He would take me to the picture show, let me go with him on his mail route in the summer, and ride me around to see some of his friends, but I had to stay in the car and read while he visited. In return, I wasn't to tell Aunt Minnie or Grannie about the bottles that collected in the back room of the barn.

And when he was "thinking" I had to leave him alone. He spent a lot of time thinking and being quiet. Some of my aunts pitied him because he must miss my mother. But when we rode around in the car, ladies liked to talk to him. Once, one of those ladies followed him out of the house, trying to catch up to him as he hurried to the car. She leaned on my car door and looked in at me. She smelled all sweaty and like the bottles in the barn. She asked, "Wouldn't you like for me to come and live with you and cook you some of them good ole apple jacks like I gave you last time?"

"No. I don't like you."

My bluntness would have make Grannie mad, but Daddy started laughing as we drove away. He laughed until he had to wipe the tears from his cheeks. He said, "I didn't know how I was going to get out of that one. Young'un, you have a way with words, and they're usually the right ones." Daddy didn't like to argue or tell people no. He always said he'd walk a mile out of his way to avoid an argument.

That worried me.

Grannie wanted to come into our house and raise me up right. She had her good points. Like when our refrigerator wore out, she gave us the one she'd had at her house. Seems like she reminded us of that all the time though.

I felt sad about Aunt Minnie leaving me, but I was more upset about Grannie moving in.

The Sunday visitors left, and I waited for somebody to tell me the latest news, but Daddy went to the barn and Aunt Minnie opened her Bible.

Aunt Minnie never talked about the Lord the way Grannie did, but she went to church every Sunday and read the Good Book a lot. When Grannie would try to stir up trouble about one thing or another, Aunt Minnie would just say, "Do unto others as you would have them do unto you." She lived quietly, the way Daddy did. I often wondered how they could be so nice with Grannie raising them, but I found out she was their step-mother. That explained everything. I knew all about step-mothers from Cinderella.

Daddy remained patient with Grannie though. He said she lived a hard life being the first generation after the Civil War when the carpetbaggers came in and took over the government and raised taxes so high that Grannie's family lost most of their land. After she married Granddaddy, she spent her whole life working to get land and good crops. Daddy said, "Hard work makes some people mean."

I didn't care much about what made her that way. I just didn't want to be on the receiving end of her meanness. I remembered the week before when she had nearly destroyed a young peach tree, tearing off a switch to whip me.

All of us cousins played ball in the backyard. We had a string ball with a rubber middle and a bat with a cracked handle. We didn't have bases but took turns hitting the ball and trying to catch it. My batting turn changed family history. Grannie was in the yard at the outside pump. She dipped snuff, and every day she would wash out her

Daddy & Aunt Minnie

spittoon. She bent over to pick it up at the same time I hit a line-drive. The ball bounced off her skinny little butt, and she came up squalling, "Ohhhhh!"

Our eyes met over the heads of my escaping cousins. I intended to be brave until she started tearing into that peach tree. I ran and hid under the front porch all afternoon, playing with doodlebugs.

After the relatives left, Grannie ended up on the front porch fussing about me to Daddy and Aunt Minnie. They almost never talked back to her.

"The older she gets the more she acts like her mama. Wild. No sense. Acts like a shiftless tenant farmer."

Nobody said anything after that. Grannie got up and went to her bedroom. Hiding under the porch, I could hear her singing, *We shall gather at the river* in that tinny little voice of hers. Daddy stopped rocking and walked to the edge of the porch. In my imagination, I could see him staring off toward the graveyard, like he did sometimes. Finally, he cleared his throat and said, "That puny little bitch is going to find herself sitting on the side of the road if she keeps running her mouth."

Pride rose up in me. My daddy was on my side. Tears rolled down my cheeks as I scrambled out from under the porch and ran to Grannie's window. At the top of my lungs, I screamed at her, "It won't do you no good to sing hymns. You're a dried up old bitch, and you're going to hell."

Before the words left my mouth good, Daddy had jumped off the porch and jerked me up by one arm and swatted me four times on the butt. But when I looked into his face, I could see a smile hiding there. I'd never been spanked before, but my feelings were not hurt because I knew Daddy and I were on the same team.

Aunt Minnie getting married changed the rules some though. I sat on the Chinaberry tree swing watching the barn. When Daddy came out, he headed straight for me. "Come on, let's go see a man about a mule." That's what he'd always say when we drove around the county roads. He parked the 1954 Willys under the bridge and we watched Little River run by. It took him a good long while to work up to it. He finally said, "I got something to tell you. I wanted to talk to you before you heard it from some of the relatives. Your Aunt Minnie is going to get married to Mr. Frank next week. She'll be moving into his house."

I didn't say anything because my breath caught in my throat. I had not heard it would be so soon. I felt him looking closely at me. He wasn't the kind of daddy that you hugged and cried into his shirt like I'd seen on the picture shows. I didn't know what to do or say. His hand dug into his pocket and pulled a handful of coins out and searched until he found an Indian-head nickel. He held it up between us.

"Now you know we are related to the Indians, right? How many books have you read about Indians?" He didn't wait for an answer but pressed on. "They had a fine way of life, but the white man took it away from them. They suffered a lot, but they didn't whine and cry about it. Look at this Indian's face." We looked at the coin together. "Life's hard sometimes, but we don't give in to it. We stay strong. See how brave his face is? I think that's what you and me ought to do. Your Aunt Minnie is mighty sad to leave you, but she's got to do what's best for her. You understand? We don't want to make her feel any worse than she already does. You agree with me? We'll be all right. I'm a good cook and you've been sweeping the floor and dusting for two or three years."

I sniffed back the threatening tears and took the coin out of his hand. I looked at the hard unemotional face of the Native American and took a deep ragged breath.

"Okay."

"Good, that's my gal. I knew you'd be all right." He put the Jeep in reverse and turned back toward Highway 222. We drove in silence all the way home, until I saw Uncle Herman's truck with some boxes in the back parked in the driveway.

"What we going to do about her?"

"Who?"

"Grannie. Everybody says she's moving in."

Something like anger flashed in Daddy's eyes and then it was gone. One hand left the steering wheel and roughly pulled down the brim of his sweat-stained grey Fedora.

Grannie stood on the back steps with her fists on her hips and mouth in a grim line across her prune face. I'd never seen her more determined.

"We went on and loaded up some of my stuff that Herman had at his house. Might as well get settled in."

Daddy stood by the driver's door of the car and I ran around to join him. They stared at each other. Suddenly, he turned to me and put his hands on my shoulders and looked directly into my eyes.

"Do you want Grannie to come and live with us?"

The answer resounded from the last time I saved him. "No, I don't like her."

Daddy stood very straight and looked back at Grannie. "There's your answer." With that, he turned and walked to the barn.

Avoiding eye contact with the furious little woman, I skipped down the driveway and around the house. Grannie yelled and fussed for a while, but I stayed clear. Then Uncle Herman's truck started and I watched him back out of the driveway with Grannie, the boxes, and the refrigerator.

What I Wish I Could Tell You
Kathryn Etters Lovatt

How hot the summer has been.
We sit on the porch swing
waiting for a breeze, but none
cuts through the honeysuckle vine.
Its insufferable sweetness gathers and hangs,
a fierce cloud without rain.

The garden peaked late this year,
now it goes too fast. Tomatoes took their time
coming in, then ripened all at once.
Early in the season, I ate them unwashed,
unsalted off the vine: their seeds
dripped off my chin into the ground.

I've had my fill, but still I take my share—
between the last good tomato of one year
and the first good one of the next
lies a whopping wait.
You, who could not wait, should remember that,
although if grace conveys to afterlife

you know nothing of last spring,
how your stomach boiled and your taste turned bitter.
We brought soft eggs, potassium broths,
hush-hush elixirs of mushrooms and peach pits.
You shook beneath the quilts and dreamed
out loud of one decent tomato,

red as a vial of blood, skin thin as your own,
stretched so tight it would shed in one long strip,
peel away like a blister. You ached
for blinding blue skies beyond your reach,
for the harvests such days produce.
You longed for times like these, afternoon

inching toward sunset's bright shudder,
a chance to witness fire
yielding to an advent of stars. Tonight,
every night, we feel the loss of you. The sky
looks pitifully bald: no rings around the moon,
no signs for us to follow.

If you can find a way, remind us, Mother,
all living things blossom and wither,
all things die and return. Tell us again
of nature's order and economy.
Promise nothing is ever wasted;
nothing, ever lost.

A Million Little Worlds
S. Jane Gari

Mountains of marbles haunted an abandoned glass factory in the West Virginia town where my stepfather was born. My stepsister and I discovered the structure while trudging the tired knolls and streets of Paden City, accusing it at every turn of not being a city at all. And then from the nothing, a factory sprouted out of an expanse of hillside and cracked concrete riddled with weeds—the stuff of dreams to us fourth and fifth-graders.

The large wooden shell of a building looked as if a modest bomb had detonated somewhere in its basement years ago, scattering millions of globes in a twenty-acre radius. Looking out at the heaps of marbles made me feel like a god scanning the universe. Countless little worlds as far as you could see. Each one slippery and smooth in your hand—until you dropped it.

The marbles were beautiful despite the weather. It was Thanksgiving weekend, and the sky adopted a steely kind of gray—muting the world and sapping its color. But even in that dimness, we could tell the marbles were special, and I couldn't wait to examine them in the light.

We ran back to my step-grandmother's house and begged for containers. We needed something to scoop up all the loot. To this day, I'm not sure if we were trespassing at the factory or not, but our childhood enthusiasm bought us a milk crate full of empty Mason jars without the third degree. So I like to assume we came by the marbles honestly.

Back at the factory, I lay atop the field of glass orbs, waving my arms and legs the way you do to make snow angels. Wriggling around made the marbles roll against my back like the gentle pressure of knuckles giving me a massage. My stepsister and I gathered our plunder, laughing like a couple of pirates who'd raided Davy Jones's locker.

I took the marbles back home to Ohio and kept the Mason jars on the floor of my closet. Then I fished out a few handfuls and placed them in a thick glass bowl swiped from the basement. I liked the way it helped the clear globes catch and scatter the light and made the solid ones shine like rare fruits.

Such possibility in a simple bowl of marbles. I didn't know what, but I knew I wanted them to be important. Even though I was only nine, I obsessed over meaning and infused my everyday objects with stories I knew or could guess at—a plant wilted from sadness; Nana's necklace kept nightmares at bay. One part of this magical thinking came from being an imaginative kid, the other from moving around so much and enduring my parents' divorce. The world really could change on a dime—or a marble. The fleeting nature of the tangible and intangible made me prone to an even mix of detachment and reverence. I wanted to save myself from the hurt of losing people and things, but I also cherished what and who I had because I knew better than to trust the illusion of permanence. If you go into the game knowing nothing is ever truly yours, it makes everything special—and you don't suffer as much.

I loved the marbles so much, I decided to give them away. Not all at once. One at a time. Every time someone new came into my life and visited my room—the sacred sanctuary of childhood and adolescent intimacy—I would offer them the bowl of marbles. "Choose one and keep it forever," I'd say. This was how my collection worked—in reverse. For every friend gained, I would send a marble out into my expanding world.

I remember every face lit up with possibility as they chose a marble from the bowl. Sometimes I could guess which one they'd pick by their personality. The clear, transparent marbles with suspended air bubbles inside went to honest and forthright people. The rainbow-swirled worlds left with the most dynamic characters. When I got older and befriended a string of dark and mysterious boys who wrote questionable poetry, they'd always eye the sparkly marbles first but end up settling for the darker opaque orbs just for show. I could have devised quite the sincerity-screening test with that bowl of marbles. It would have saved me some heartache.

Wherever I moved, I took the marbles with me, and I watched my supply dwindle with each new person I'd meet. I brought them to college, to a house in England, to apartments in New York. One by one—I gave them away.

The most satisfying part about the marbles was running into people I hadn't seen in years and learning they'd kept them. They incorporated them into jewelry or keychains, or stashed them among trinkets in a jewelry box, a memory to hold and roll around in the palm for a while. The aftermath of college in the pre-internet world separated me from many friends, but some of them were returned to me with the dawn of social media. One such reunion resulted in some actual face-time with a high school friend, one who'd chosen a brightly-colored marble and stood by his decision. He showed me his wallet and the deep half-moon groove his well-loved marble carved there.

"Even when we couldn't find each other, I had a piece of you with me," he said.

And that sealed my reasoning. In giving them away, I'd built bridges out of marbles forever connecting me to the people who meant something to me, even if only for a moment. I'd invited them into my space to share time and talk about the world. I'd given them a talisman, and they'd kept and treasured it.

After eighteen years of giving, there was only one marble left.

It sat in a bowl in my bedroom of the apartment I shared with my cousin. For a year, I didn't meet anyone new. I started to grow superstitious. Maybe this one last marble meant my circle of friends was finally closed. I was still single, and the thought scared me. I was twenty-six and could already feel the narrowing and tightening effect of "the real world" on my social life.

And then there was Brendon.

I'd met Brendon before. Many times. One of my best friends, Greg, had gone to high school with him, so we'd run into each other at the same parties. His superhero's jawline was permanently inhabited by a five o'clock shadow, and he sported black, long eyelashes any woman would envy. But they worked on him. They worked on me. His stare could hold me paralyzed while I struggled to pay attention to the words falling from his mouth in thick New York waves.

Brendon asked Greg to bring me to his parents' house for his sister's graduation party. Brendon and I sipped rum and Cokes and pretended to argue about the best spot to view the Long Island sunset because we were both too shy to admit we were asking each other for a date. We just needed to settle the argument, that's all. I'd go see his spot, and he would see mine. He would come to my apartment the next night to ante up on Part I of Operation Sunset.

My spot lay two blocks away at Morgan Park on the Long Island Sound. We could walk there together. I fussed over three sundresses before deciding on the brown one peppered with turquoise flowers and then paired it with a ponytail and sneakers so I didn't look like I had tried too hard. But I worked on that ponytail for a good thirty minutes.

When Brendon got to my place, we walked to the beach and set up camp atop a wall fashioned to mimic the turrets of a medieval castle. The perch offered an ample slice of Long Island Sound and faced due west. I won the argument as the sky ripened in blood oranges striped in purple clouds. When it all faded to black, we kept watch over the Sound and talked about our dreams. After several hours, the mosquitoes and threat of daybreak finally drove us back to my apartment.

"I have something for you," I said to him.

"You do?"

"It's in my bedroom."

"Oh really?" The playful smirk in his voice was almost my undoing.

"It's not like *that*. Come on, I'll show you."

I led him to my room and handed him the bowl. "This is the last marble. I guess it's been waiting for you." I explained how I'd come by my collection and how he was the final recipient of my last little world.

He lifted the sunset-colored marble from the bowl. "It looks like an orange Jupiter. Even has a big spot like Jupiter."

"You know, scientists think that spot is an enormous storm that's been raging for hundreds of years." I gripped the edge of my desk with both hands to stop myself from rocking on my heels like a little kid, a habit that belied my excitement. Mysteries like the longevity of Jupiter's storm got me riled up about being alive, but I didn't want to come off as too strange. I was giving him a marble I'd just said had been waiting for him. I figured that was enough quirkiness for the time being.

"Hundreds of years?" he said. "That's amazing." He placed the marble in his palm like a living thing—like a tiny world waiting to be explored.

I didn't have to wait for a chance meeting to find out what happened to Brendon's talisman. We were married nearly three years to the day I'd given him my last marble. But still, in the swirl of life and jobs and child-rearing, I hadn't thought about "Jupiter" in years—until one winter afternoon when we were rummaging through the master bedroom closet for the pre-Christmas purge. As we decided which sweaters would be donated, and which dresses might be worn again, we also raked through keepsake boxes. Brendon pulled a necklace from a swirl of lanyards and old coins. And there it was.

"You still have that?" I asked.

"Of course I do," he said. "I made a pouch for it, remember?" He peeled open the crude, tiny pocket of leather attached to the necklace and showed me the marble I hadn't seen in more than a decade.

"Jupiter," he said, smiling.

I felt myself rocking on my heels. And I didn't stop.

A Place I Belonged
John W. Aldrich

In 1999, my parents and I faced a dilemma. Up until that year, I attended public school with few problems. I averaged A or B letter grades in almost every subject, absent hardly more than two or three days. My teachers' personal comments on report cards included "very well-behaved student," "polite young man," or "wish the class were full of students like John." All appeared well.

However, a major concern presented itself going forward. My adventures in elementary school would end with the spring semester. The middle grades loomed on the horizon—an arena full of raging hormones, physical and emotional changes, and hardships like peer pressure, demanding responsibilities, and questions of identity. Unfortunately, my parents' careers landed them like bookends on either side of where I needed them to be. Mom taught fourth grade at the local elementary school and always had a hand in who instructed me. Dad ruled high school algebra and geometry. However, neither parent held any expertise beyond their narrowly defined niches. This time, they could not transition with me to the next tier of the educational hierarchy.

Dad genuinely wanted to teach me, believing he was my mathematical messiah. Math was always a subject I loathed deeply and therefore performed poorly. I loved and admired Dad, but I absolutely *hated* math. Despite all my accomplishments, including a prized ribbon for high achievement in the Accelerated Reader Program, math was my great disaster. I could not wrap my head around the simplest problems, and I struggled to memorize tables, still counted on my fingers, and felt utterly daunted using a calculator.

From as far back as I can remember, my parents kept saying, "A good education is invaluable." Dad received his Masters from South Carolina's most prestigious military university, the Citadel—in mathematics. At age twenty-one, Mom earned her Bachelors in Early Childhood Education over a three-year period. Both of them continued to teach, each for over thirty years, all the while juggling a family and tending to aging parents. Mom started my college plan before I was born. Both taught me how to read at age three, encouraging me to sound out unfamiliar words and associate with pictures. With unflagging attention, they instilled basic virtues in me.

However, they also worried about me, concerned over a future I didn't fully understand. They wanted their son to have the opportunities they did—including a chance to obtain a college degree and a career. My mom was especially keen on this point.

The local middle school remained the obvious choice of where I'd attend, because of distance—only a five-minute drive from our house. In my town, the main learning institutions were located side-by-side on the same street, just outside the suburbs. I visited the buildings and got the whiff of a fast-paced curriculum, a variety of students, some dedicated and homely like me, others dressed in black with long or dyed hair, many of different races and cultures, a few familiar faces, and a few who obviously didn't care to be there. All of them busily zoomed back and forth between lunch and classes.

When I arrived at Dad's school, I saw much the same thing, except the teens were older and somewhat rougher, and the student numbers went up—over a thousand attended. Both places offered athletic scholarships in basketball or football and sports accolades. Caring essentially nothing for sports of any kind, never desiring to compete—I found myself left out.

As a quiet, obedient boy who preferred to study, I imagined being tempted and hounded by older, tougher teens who might lead me down a path I did not want to travel. Ostracized and abused for my gawky looks or for my soft-spoken ways and private nature, I would be left to fend for myself.

I felt like yelling, *"Can anybody hear me? Can anybody see? Please! Somebody save me from becoming a lumped-in number!"*

Fortunately, Mom found an answer—the only one available. I would have to attend a private school, a college-prep academy.

Holding no clue beyond what I'd seen in movies or read in fiction, I wanted to know as much as possible.

"Tell me all about what my new school will be like," I said to her one night while helping prepare supper. I imagined something akin to Britney Spears's voluptuous Catholic school or a grueling all-male military institution where everyone wore uniforms and repeated "Sir, yes sir!" when addressed.

"Well, college prep means you'll be *prepared* for more school after you graduate. They'll have smaller class sizes, a nice family atmosphere, and you'll have better one-on-one help for your math. I went to a private academy, myself—an all-girls school in North Carolina called Vardell Hall. We'll check out a few to find a good fit," Mom said.

We started our search in early spring. Hammond, on the far side of Columbia, was our first choice. I thought immediately of the child-like, slightly insane tycoon who pumped money into a prehistoric amusement park from Michael Crichton's famous book. Adoring dinosaurs, fantastical creatures, and everything to do with *Jurassic Park*, I naively thought Richard Attenborough's eccentric character, John F. Hammond, founded the school. However, James H. Hammond founded Hammond School in 1966 as a private pre-K through twelfth grade learning center.

I thought I would fit right in. Upscale, with the (then) latest technology verging on the new century, state-of-the-art computer labs, clean classrooms with plenty of supplies and renovations, the campus grounds sprawled before us. Mom and Dad were thoroughly awed, and so was I.

We spoke with a vigorous and friendly guidance counselor, laughing and joking a great deal, which made me feel at ease. I followed all of them around the great rooms and hallways and met some of the faculty who would be teaching me. They looked impressive, dressed in suits and neckties. A bearded man taught engagingly from notes as we sat in on his class. He shook my hand and gave me a wide smile when we left.

On the way home, I kept thinking how much both of my parents loved it—and how much I would enjoy learning in this amazing place. True, I did feel nervous. The unfamiliar faces, the new names, getting around a spread-out campus, all presented challenges, but I was confident. Mom said she always became nervous at the beginning of every school year.

A trial experiment would prove ideal for me to experience the ins and outs of Hammond School. I agreed to spend a whole day with kids my own age, in my future grade. I would hang out with them in the classroom, and on the grounds as one of the team, a member of the academy.

Although a brilliant idea in theory, it totally backfired in reality.

Excited and energetic, I arrived ready to begin one of the best days of my life in my new-found prep school. Our teacher introduced me to the class as a guest "sitting in with us today. I want you all to show him your best behavior and make him feel welcome." They did so wonderfully. Hardly anyone spoke out of turn, and only once did the teacher call for attention.

So I obediently listened as she went through lesson-by-lesson and subject-by-subject. Much of the material was standard and familiar to me. For a half hour, the kids quietly worked in their workbooks.

One of them later voiced a question, which the teacher reworked into a statement to make a point. On the whole, the morning went by very orderly, and the students were all alert and sharp.

Knowing I could ask anything I wished and express my opinion freely felt good, but still I sensed something big lacking here—and I couldn't express it accurately. I regarded myself as an outsider, though I didn't know why.

Later, we went out to the playground, an activity I wondered about because I had heard middle-schoolers never climbed jungle gyms or negotiated slides. Once I entered middle school, I expected to sit around and talk after meals in the manner of grown-ups—I guessed I would discuss paying bills, cooking, and cleaning. I would behave like an adult. So why were we out here hopping, skipping, and jumping around instead of in the courtyard talking? I attempted to ask our teacher but was cut off by the morning bell.

Anne Lamott wrote in her book, *Bird by Bird*, how you can tell a lot about someone from the contents of his or her school lunch. The kids of Hammond ate a wide variety of foods, including salads and chicken on the bone. All of our lunches were eaten in the same classroom. *Odd*, I thought. *We should go to the cafeteria.* Only Hammond *had* no cafeteria. The tour had not included one; students brought their meals with them and ate inside the classrooms.

I tried a bit of conversation at mealtime, trying several kids to see if they liked stuff like monster movies, reading, or writing. Apparently, no one did. I looked sheepishly at my PB & J sandwich, and bottled water, and realized I was like an animal out of its habitat, a "stranger in a strange land," as Robert Heinlein wrote in his book about a Martian visiting Earth.

My alien status cemented itself permanently (and ironically) in the last period of the day—art class. At first, I thought we would find some common ground. I had entertained myself until early adolescence with elaborate daydreams, games, and hundreds of action figures; I loved drawing detailed sketches and paintings of characters and monsters from my favorite movies and stories. One of them even won an award and was displayed over our mantelpiece. Like Dad's mother before me, who painted pictures and sold them, I naturally thought art class should have helped me blend right in.

Wrong! These kids seemed beyond gifted. One girl drew a beautiful monarch butterfly, much greater than life size, full of exotic colors, intricate details, and contours. Another boy had drawn a full-color tiger sketch, which reminded me of everything in photos I'd seen at the zoo and nothing of Hobbes from the Bill Watterson comic, (these strips were taped to the art room door). Still more penciled *Dragonball Z* characters—a popular animated fantasy franchise. The artists of Hammond left me in the dust.

When the day ended, I fled campus, upset at how disappointing the experience had been. Such lofty expectations, only to have them plummet in a matter of hours. Both the kids and teachers lacked something—something crucial I needed. I tried to express this to my parents, but could not. I came to the conclusion Hammond was not where I belonged, but even so, I returned one last time.

"The Big One" (what I called the entrance exam) determined if I would be accepted into the fold. We sat in a huge, plain classroom, where the same bearded man who taught art class administered the series of timed tests. I struggled like that idiot custodian of the 1990s comedy film series, Jim Varney's Ernest P. Worrell, to just break the seal of the absolute *book* he had given me.

After some delay, I began the exam, which followed an administered orally-given outline much like the infamous college PACT tests of the time. I got through the English fairly well in a series of starts and stops at our instructor's direction, but got hung up on the math portion in another volley of mental firecrackers. The English portion blew by easily enough; however, trouble brewed in the math section—just as I expected. I worked slowly and gave my best effort, but the questions were sophisticated and dryly academic.

Over four hours transpired—and I wanted to *expire*. At 12:00 noon, sticky with sweat, and feeling sick to my stomach, I handed in my exam and left the building, thinking I would love never having to endure testing again.

The results came in about a week later. My grasp of English was rated satisfactory, but science and math were not rated at all! I only answered some twenty of over fifty questions—a classic portrait of my underdeveloped skills in these fields. Ultimately, I flunked the entrance exam. However, I was relieved. No more journeys into Columbia traffic, no more treks ninety minutes from home. Back to square one, time was running thin. Summer was beginning, and I had not been placed.

I would have to go to school, but where? We searched and searched. Mom thumbed through catalogs and made phone calls; Dad Yahooed and talked to parents and other kids. Then, like treasure hunters digging holes in the desert, we hit gold.

The latest lead took us not back into the heart of the city, but far into the rolling hills of Santee, to a border town in the wilderness, near the city of Sumter, a place called Rembert. *This is more like it*, I thought, staring excitedly out the backseat window.

Evidently a school was located out there, hidden behind a grove of trees, a school that sat on a sloping land rise, nicknamed "The Hill"; the official title, we discovered, was an acronym. The sign said WELCOME TO TSA, HOME OF THE GENERALS.

We met with the headmaster, a big man with a friendly handshake. His assistant gave us a tour. The campus was not especially lavish, but comfortably rural and catered to students from a wide range of socio-economic backgrounds whose parents could afford the modest tuition. Some of the teachers and students talked with slight accents, others with a definite twang, and everyone was friendly and gracious, acting with Southern charm and hospitality. The clean buildings, the small courtyard, and the legendary cafeteria food looked attractive on our inspection.

"You'll be sure to try Miss Marvell's gravy biscuits. They melt right in your mouth," said Mrs. Schmeling, the upper-school guidance counselor.

I thought: *Yes! Home-cooked meals away from home!*

In addition to good meals, if I should elect Thomas Sumter Academy to be my home school, I would get excellent lessons: the basic reading, writing, and arithmetic, of course, but a slew of everything else imaginable as well. From all the arts, music, and theater, to the sciences and theology, no limits existed in any field I wished to explore. *Can't go wrong here,* I thought. I liked the arts already because I drew, sketched, and painted, and listened to classical music, even at age twelve. So the place cast a charm over me. I would learn what I loved.

Also, TSA had an old-fashioned country draw—the attending students were sons and daughters of farmers and teachers. Many of the families who sent their kids there had connections back to the academy as faculty, like Mrs. Richardson, and Mr. and Mrs. Minton. At some point they would teach me, along with their children. The student numbers were much smaller here—around six hundred attended.

At last, I realized Hammond School did not have the deeply personal touch I needed. At TSA they were family—not only friends, teachers, students or faculty. They made me feel like a valued member.

I prayed to pass the entrance exam.

"The Big One II," my second shot at getting in, would prove my case. I took the test with a few others in the tiny lower-school library. "Take as long you want," our monitor said, so I spent over an hour seated in silence. I remember writing a descriptive essay about my shoe, a blue-black New Balance. The last question asked about my favorite book and/or movie, so I wrote at length about the moral questions raised in *Jurassic Park*. My results came back satisfactory in all categories, but, even so, I lacked crucial mathematic word-problem-solving skills. An algebra teacher named Mr. Newman would help fix this. I was accepted to Thomas Sumter Academy and would begin classes in the autumn.

I still remember the trophy case in the main hallway. The golden awards sparkled; the medallions glittered as the sunlight caught them. The floors, made of actual pine boards, creaked underfoot. The walls were lined with portraits of all the headmasters in the academy's nearly forty-year history. Their faces beamed down as I approached.

General Thomas Sumter

I stood frozen, gazing upward. A soldier's framed portrait reared above, glistening. *Whoa.* I was standing before the portrait of General Thomas Sumter, whose illustrious name the school and nearby city still bear. The man, the myth, the one everyone kept referring to, arose squarely in front of me in full battle regalia, his hand resting on the hilt of his sheathed rapier. He looked dignified and true, every bit the humble warrior, the original patriot.

Late afternoon sunlight slanted behind me and glowed on the wise face of the general; his eyes shone upon me with promise. *Welcome home,* they said.

At last, a place I belonged!

Phoenix Out of Ashes
Ashley M. Carmichael

Everything is a blur. My heart pounds. Nothing is familiar. Panic sets in as realization strikes...I'm lost.

When I was three my family took a trip to Disney World. We stepped through the entrance, and enchanted, I pushed my way through the crowd. My destination: Cinderella's castle. Soon a sea of faces swam around me, and not one was familiar. In a place where dreams are supposed to come true, a little girl stood alone and scared.

Ten years later, I was lost in another blur of faces. I wandered aimlessly through high school, known only as "Katherine's Sister" or "The Middle Carmichael Kid" or my personal favorite, "Hey Girl."

"It's the best time of your life," they said. Well, whoever *they* were, *they* never had *The Nightmare.*

Flames leapt from the center of the pit every night, licking at the dry vegetation. Crisp, brown grass, leaves, and branches fed the wrath of the fire beneath. I held fast to the one green bush on the side of the hill, but my strength faded fast. Trapped in this pit, I heard voices echoing—voices of people I knew I loved, but couldn't quite recognize. Were they leaping out of the fire or falling into the flames?

Turning to look, my grip loosened. I squeezed my eyes tight and swallowed a scream, then I woke up.

Always at the same time: 2 a.m.

By the end of my second or third week of ninth grade, exhaustion replaced common sense. All I wanted was one good night's sleep. Instead, my band instructor made after school practice mandatory. So I was stuck after school practicing an instrument for which I had no talent or passion. Trumpet sectionals. At least I had my friends even though sleep had fled.

One afternoon, both our section leaders were noticeably absent, so our drum major, Patrick, stayed to whip us into shape. This handsome senior, a feature writer for the school paper, one of the few leaders people actually listened to, grabbed my attention. But then, everyone knew Patrick. I kept my head down, followed directions, and avoided eye contact. I knew Patrick, but he didn't care to know me. No one did. I was 'Hey Girl' for a reason.

Sectionals lasted an hour, which translated into high school vernacular meant five minutes of work for every fifteen-minute break. The three of us girls talked in a huddle, pretending to ignore the immature antics of boys who surrounded us. We were outnumbered, but we didn't mind.

During one of the many breaks, a sharp noise startled me. I looked up just in time to see a stupid six-inch plastic chicken flying toward my head. I ducked, and it landed harmlessly on the grass. Heat crept up the back of my neck as I glared at the guys, meeting Patrick's laughing brown-eyed gaze.

"What was that for?" I asked, one hand on my hip the way a sassy fourteen-year-old is supposed to demand answers.

He shrugged. I rolled my eyes and threw it back at him. He caught it, then smirked. I turned my back.

"What are you doing tonight?" Jennifer asked.

"I'm not sure. Katherine said she's going to the mall with Kelly and I can go if I want to, but…"

Ka-thump.

Elizabeth, Jennifer, and I stared at the plastic chicken at our feet. Without waiting for either of the other girls to close their mouths, I picked the chicken up and tossed it out into the field, far from the snickering boys beside us.

"Don't you like the chicken?" Patrick asked. He stood behind my shoulder and my eyes widened—I hadn't expected him to get so close.

Heat spread rapidly from the back of my neck to my face as Patrick jogged off to retrieve the plastic projectile. Elizabeth poked me in the ribs.

"He is so flirting with you!" she whispered.

"Shut up," I murmured. "He is not."

Elizabeth thought that if a guy bumped into you at the mall he was flirting, but I knew better. Patrick was a senior; he wouldn't flirt with Katherine's sister. With Katherine? Sure, but not with her nerdy little sister.

As it turns out, I was right. What seemed like flirting turned out to be a challenge. One that Patrick unknowingly issued and I unwittingly accepted.

A week later, because it was the nineties and pre-text messaging days, I logged into my AOL instant messenger while I worked on a science paper. I was waiting for Jennifer and Elizabeth who were in my class. I figured we could chat about the assignment and finish it together. But neither Elizabeth nor Jennifer messaged me that night. Instead, PJBburn13 did.

PJBburn13: Sorry if I embarrassed you the other day.

I knew all about the horrors of talking to strangers online, but even though I didn't know who PJBburn13 was, he seemed to know me. What had he done to embarrass me? That week alone I had fallen down the hill and gotten mud all over my backside, tripped over a power cord in Spanish class, and been hit with a volleyball in gym. Embarrassment was kind of my best friend.

ACBlondey: Um, that's okay—no biggie…who is this?

I didn't know one word could stop my heart. But it did.

PJBburn13: Patrick =)

My hands shook as I typed. I couldn't believe he wanted to talk to me. To me.

For weeks, we talked back and forth on messenger. He read Hemingway, listened to REM and the Beatles, effortlessly quoted Shakespeare, Plato, and John Lennon. With each conversation, he peeled away my protective shell and exposed a vulnerable side of me I didn't even know existed. The side where I questioned everything I ever thought I believed. I would ask a question: Do you believe in absolute truth? And he would answer with insight that didn't seem real.

PJBburn13: I believe that there is an underlying force in nature that gives guidance as to what is fundamentally 'right' and fundamentally 'wrong', but I don't believe that it is possible to separate things into two opposing categories. That makes life 2-dimensional and I firmly believe that it isn't.

My heart would pound. It didn't add up to me, so I would go searching for my own answers, digging deeper and deeper into what I truly believed. He would challenge me, and I would freeze, unable to respond because I didn't actually know the answer.

A voice, his voice, echoed in my mind as I clung to a belief that had deep roots, but wasn't actually a part of me. And my strength was fading.

What I thought was just a high school crush, turned out to be much more than puppy love. My friendship with Patrick was a message from God.

The night before his graduation I had *The Nightmare* again, but it changed. The flames burned just as hot, the voices cried just as loud, but when sweat broke out on my forehead, I didn't wake up. Instead I heard a voice say two words: *Let go.*

Terrified, I gripped the bush harder and shook my head, but the words, soft and reassuring, repeated: *Let go.*

I felt the heat from the flames all around me.

Taking a deep breath, I finally did let go.

I watched myself fall into the pit, into the fire, and disappear.

Instead of screaming, I woke up feeling peace. Reborn. A phoenix from the ashes. What I had been trying to escape for so long, the fire—those voices—was what I'd needed to embrace. I realized fire doesn't always destroy, sometimes it refines.

For the first time I understood God. He spoke to me.

As I lay in the dark, staring up at the ceiling, counting breaths and moments between the ticks of time, I listened, really listened. Over and over I prayed for God to speak again, and just when I was about to fall back to sleep, I heard His voice. Not audibly and maybe even a faded part of the dream, but it was clear: *Pray for him.*

As a child lost in the crowd, I sobbed until a friendly hand reached down, picked me up, and comforted me. This stranger stood me up on the top of a bench so my family could find me. Ten years passed and physically I grew, but spiritually I was the same three-year-old, lost and alone. Ironically, my agnostic friend took me by the hand and stood me on a bench until God found me. God reminded me He is the one who cherishes me—even when I wander off.

My Sister, the Captain/Colonel
Brenda Bevan Remmes (as told to her by her husband Bill)

My sister Betty is ten years older and grew up on one farm or the other. In Iowa, land and roads are laid out in square miles—640 acres

Mom, Betty, Bill, and John

per land warrant. All roads run north-south and east-west. Farmers who don't own property usually rent land in 160 acres segments. The farmer pays 50% of whatever their cash crop produces to the landowners. (Today's market usually requires a cash rental in lieu of percentages.) If there is a house on the property then it is commonly required that the tenant farmer live in the house as part of the rental.

To this day, farmers re-negotiate their rental property every March. Landowners obviously want a farmer who will bring in the highest cash crop. Tenant farmers continue to look for better farm land or a better house for their family. In past times that would include one with electricity or in-door plumbing. Accordingly, my mom and dad began a series of moves during their nineteen years of farming together.

We never had indoor plumbing while we lived on the farms and if you don't think it's cold in Iowa when you have to run back and forth to an outhouse, then you've never experienced an Iowa winter. John and I decided early on to simply pee out the upstairs bedroom window. Mom figured out what was causing the yellow streak down the side of the house and put a stop to that. Think we had a pee pot from then on.

We bathed on Saturdays in an oval galvanized washtub. Warm water would be poured out from the reservoir tank attached to the wood stove and the oldest member of the family got to bathe first, working down one by one to the youngest. Sometimes the water was so dirty by the last scrub that a baby might get lost in it. Hence the saying, *Don't throw the baby out with the bathwater.*

I sort of envied my cousins, the Mohatts, who reversed the process and bathed starting from the youngest up. Only problem was Dick, who got first dibs, used to pee in the water just to spite his older brother, Jerry. His dad figured it out, though, and put an abrupt stop to Dick's attempts to get revenge. We both had older-brother problems.

Only four main roads were paved in Crawford County in the 30s and 40s (Highways #59, #30, #141, and #39). Everything else was hard dirt. In the winters many roads became impassable with the snow. In the spring when the topsoil would thaw and couldn't drain because of the frozen ground beneath, they were a mess.

A two-mile hike to school was considered reasonable for elementary school children and I never remember missing a day of school due to weather. Years later after relocating to the South with my wife, I have yet to acclimate to how a whole region of the country can become paralyzed over a mere inch or less of snow.

John and I were already born and living in the Coleman house by Arion when Mom and Dad needed to decide where to send Betty to live if she was going to go to high school. After eighth grade there was no bus service to the high schools in town. My parents must have been apprehensive, but Teresa and Vince Mohatt came to the rescue and she stayed with them during the first year in exchange for some babysitting with Dick and Jerry, most assuredly a challenge.

Her second and third years of high school were in Manning with a family she helped with minor household duties. By Betty's senior year, Mom trusted her to get an apartment in Denison with a cousin. When Dad died, she had already moved out and spent very little time with us. John was ten and I was eight.

Mom was relieved when Betty got a job with Safeway after graduation. By this time Grandma and Grandpa Laubscher and our family lived in Denison and Betty was back with us.

Betty was much older than John and me—she turned eight the same day that John was born. One aunt commented on how nice it was to have gotten a baby brother for her birthday and Betty said that the only thing she'd wanted was a cake.

Betty and Mom had one of those push-tug relationships. They weren't always sure what to do with one another. Dad played cards and checkers with Betty. Together they'd listen to the baseball games. He loved baseball. Kept telling John if he'd practice running as fast as the horse, he could play on one of the big teams one day.

Mom tried to teach Betty how to cook and complained that she even burned the bacon. But Mom did teach her how to work hard, as she did all of us, and how to handle money. Betty knew early on that if she ever wanted to leave Denison she'd have to figure out how to do it herself.

Betty saved her money and worked her way through nursing school in three years; despite the fact that one of her teachers confided in her she didn't think she was nursing material. Betty took a job at St. Joseph's Hospital in Omaha and passed the State Boards in Nebraska. But she still wanted to see other parts of the country and the military seemed a good option. In fact, the recruiters flocked to her. The economy was good. The world was at peace. Why not let someone else pay for her travel plans?

The Army tried to entice her into their olive green uniforms, but Betty didn't think she looked particularly good in green. The Navy was out because she couldn't swim. An Air Force recruiter happened to catch her with her best friend, Marialice, on the same day and promised them that they could be stationed together. That was all she needed to hear; Betty joined the Air Force in 1958, and left Denison, Iowa behind.

She and Marialice started their careers together at Maxwell Air Force Base in Montgomery, Alabama. During the next twenty-five years, Betty served in Germany, Kansas, California, Alaska, Vietnam, Topeka, Pennsylvania, San Antonio, Texas and North Dakota. In 1981 she ended up at Luke Air Force Base in Phoenix, Arizona, and stayed. She had completed a BSN degree and rose to the level of Colonel. My mother always thought "Captain" sounded more important than "Colonel," so even after all those promotions Mom always introduced Betty to her friends as, "my daughter, Captain Betty Remmes."

Colonel Betty Remmes

What I Learned from a Severe TBI
Vanessa Friedrich

Tied down to a hospital bed, I moaned and cried trying to wiggle free.

"Haaaalooooo! Haaaaalooooooo! Anybody?" Suddenly my mother leaned over me.

What was she doing here? Shouldn't she be in Germany? And where was I anyway? This didn't make sense at all!

"The doctors want to transfer you to a different hospital, which specializes in your kind of injury. Is that OK with you?" my mother asked me in my native language.

I nodded, not even knowing what injury she talked about, and drifted back into unconsciousness, a place I much preferred to be.

Weeks later, I learned that Anatole, the horse I had galloped and jumped over hurdles one morning at the track, took a misstep, stumbled, and fell, which had left me unconscious with a severe traumatic brain injury. To my relief, Anatole stayed unharmed and continued his racing career successfully. I was happy for him, but also wondered: What about my own racing career?

My shaved head and long scars indicated the craniotomy where a neurosurgeon had taken a bone flap out of my skull to give the brain room to swell and avoid brain damage. For that reason I was required to wear one of those ugly plastic safety helmets at all times. Not only did my head get hot and sweaty underneath, I also hoped that no one would ever see me with that ugly thing on my head.

And why did they put me into a wheelchair during the daytime? Was there something wrong with my legs too? Then again, I appreciated the wheelchair for the time being, since I felt too weak to stand or to walk on my own. It seemed almost unbearable to sit up all day. All I wanted was to lie down and rest, logging out for a while, hoping the next time I woke up life would be again like I used to love it: filled with laughter, friends, horses, and the race track with all its excitement.

Because of terrible coughing attacks accompanied with gasping for air, breathing wasn't easy either. Despite the fact I already had a breathing tube in my throat, which not only looked, but also felt creepy, especially when holding and pressuring air to try to have a bowel movement, I could feel air escaping through the hole in my throat. More than just once a day, the filter would fall off and needed to be screwed back on. It irritated me every time that there was such a thing that could be screwed back onto the front of my throat.

The tracheostomy, where the doctor had made a cut underneath my vocal cords into the windpipe allowing air to enter the lungs, needed to be redone because of growing scar tissue. This time the doctor disconnected my vocal cords to prevent that from happening again. That procedure shut me up for six weeks. Not even a whisper came out of my mouth. Left with my own dreadful thoughts, pen and paper became a necessity to make communication possible. I waited for the day the doctor would give me my voice back and I would be able to ask for some clarity about my situation.

After the craniotomy, a bump had formed at the left side of my head, which kept swelling, and jiggled uncontrollably with every movement. In another surgery the neurosurgeon drilled burr holes into the bump to drain the collected fluid so that my deformed head would shrink back to its original size and, if for no other reason, the ugly safety helmet would continue to fit.

After all the medical intervention and five months of speech, occupational, and physical therapy, I regained strength and balance. The missing bone piece from my skull was replaced. I traded the safety helmet for a wool cap, looking more like a cancer patient waiting for hair to grow back.

Day after day, week after week, and month after month, I searched for someone to blame before I finally gave in and believed that God came through and protected me for a reason. Now the more important question became: *Where do I go from here?*

Despite my physical and mental recovery, I had turned into a complete emotional wreck. Returning to where I had been didn't seem possible—or so I was told. Due to steroids and other medications I had gained over forty pounds, which prevented my reentry into the world of horse racing. The excess weight inhibited me from doing what I loved most and left me feeling unworthy and unattractive. Suicide as a complete check-out and the final solution for my misery sounded more and more appealing.

But something inside me wasn't ready to call it quits and say the final goodbye. I surely wanted to ride horses again, feel the sunshine warming my skin, breathe in the fresh morning air, and show the world I still had something to contribute.

I channeled all my energy into finding a new path. A friend recommended a career as a therapeutic riding instructor. *But was it possible—or even realistic—to start a new career in that field? And how would I get there?*

This time my four-legged therapists helped to find the answer. In equine assisted therapy, an activity that included my "old" and my "new" world (and how to get from one to the other), the horses gave me the idea that there was plenty of room in-between, and that it was OK for me to not already be exactly where I wanted to be. They showed me how important it was to stay calm, focused and enjoy the journey. And most of all they reminded me once again to live in the present moment—yesterday was nothing more than a memory; while tomorrow was nothing but a dream.

With determination and focus, I was able to stay productive but calm. With time, newly learned patience, the ability to take life day by day, and the assurance of being perfectly guided, I would conquer the mountain that seemed too high to climb in the first place.

There was so much more to learn from horses, I realized, than just enjoying the thrill of going fast.

Vagabond Gypsy

Lyrics, Paddy Bell

> Tendrils tangle,
> circle, spiral,
> wander between, betwixt.
> Ramble, scramble,
> wonder what's near now, what's next.
> Flights of fancy guide her,
>
> Coiling, curling,
> which way, won't say,
> mischievous cravings untamed.
> Blissful beauty,
> sweet jasmine glory unchained.
> Fancy flights delight her.
>
> Vagabond gypsy vine,
> bangles of gold design.
> Brilliant blooms
> fade too soon,
> short, sweet, her lifetime.
>
> Mountains down to the sea,
> trellising whimsically.
> Vagabond, here then gone.
> Fancy free.

Under The Wateree River Bridge
Nick West

I thought all I needed was a good pair of glasses.

After weeks of tests, my ophthalmologist said, "Nick, I have some bad news. You have a brain tumor."

Was I going to die at twenty-six? Would I get to hold my unborn child?

I felt as if I had been punched in the stomach. My wife and I sat there in the parking lot, attempting to get a grip on what we'd heard. We didn't speak on the drive home.

Over the next ten days I attempted to shield Ann from seeing the fear and anxiety that flooded every moment of my day. I'm sure she did the same for me. Time after time I walked into the house to see her staring out the window.

The night before we left for Duke, I sat alone in the den cradling my seven-month-old daughter Caroline. *Would this be the last time I held my precious little girl?* Before Ann walked into the room, I regained my composure, but that night, I wore the sheets out tossing and twisting and pleading with God.

The four-hour drive to Duke was silent; we were both in a pensive mood.

138

"The thing is," I told her, "I feel fine." Other than my minor visual problems, I suffered no other symptoms than occasional severe headaches.

When I arrived at Duke for my initial appointment with the neurosurgeon, it was apparent he was a no-nonsense man. In a matter of minutes, he diagnosed my problem.

"Go home," he said, "and be back here in ten days. We'll need at least two weeks prior to surgery to run tests."

"It took four hours to drive up here, Dr. Odom," I said. "Is there any way I can go to the hospital today or tomorrow and get this over with?"

He put his hand on my shoulder. "Son, there's a sixty percent chance you're going to die on the operating table. Go get your affairs in order."

"What will happen if I decide not to have the surgery?" I asked.

"In six months you'll be blind and in two years you'll be dead," Dr. Odom said.

When I walked out into the waiting room, Ann could see I was shaken. She wanted to know everything the surgeon had said. As we drove home, I told her most of the details, but not that I might die on the operating table.

"I need a will and a power of attorney, and I need to get you signed onto my farm checking account."

***

The day we left to check me into Duke, we dropped Caroline off at a friend's house. Once we arrived, tests began immediately. They didn't let up until 11:30 p.m. the night before surgery two weeks later.

During the eight-hour operation, Ann waited with my parents in my hospital room. A nurse came in and placed a brown paper bag on the bedside table.

"What's in the bag?" Ann asked.

"Your husband's hair."

"Why?"

"If your husband dies, you don't want to bury him bald."

Ann would tell me much later that the nurse left before they could respond.

***

After surgery, I fell into a deep coma and remained there for three weeks. A semi-coma followed for five weeks. For those eight weeks, Ann stayed at my side from morning until ten every night.

In the semi-coma, I began to dream.

My brain incorporated the tubes and machines that were keeping me alive into a strange story: still hooked up and with all my doctors and nurses accompanying me, I boarded a commercial bus. I believed the bus was taking me home, and the sight of the of the Wateree River Bridge, which I often crossed, convinced me I was right. However, in the dream, we never made it to the other side, but careened off the bridge. There we all waited.

Every day, I aroused to some level of consciousness before the surgeons' morning rounds. He would examine me as usual, but before he left he never failed to ask, "Mr. West, do you know where you are?"

My response was always the same. "I'm under the Wateree River Bridge."

Finally, I began to suspect that the doctor wanted a different answer.

One morning, when he asked his question, I told him what I thought he wanted to hear. "I'm at Duke Hospital," I said. As he walked away, I added, "But I'm really under the Wateree Bridge."

He turned and pointed his finger at me. "Don't be a smartass," he said.

I began to realize I actually *was* at Duke Hospital. That is when I started to improve, and soon I was well enough to go home.

The day of surgery, eight-inches of snow covered the ground; the day I left Duke, the grass was green, and the flowers were blooming. I felt like Rip Van Winkle.

Our daughter Caroline was with Ann's parents, and when we stopped to pick her up, our little girl would have nothing to do with us. I had on a green surgical cap, so I could understand why she shied away from me, but she didn't want Ann to hold her either. We realized she had forgotten who we were. We ended up spending the night with Ann's parents and brought Caroline home the next morning. Our pastor, Reverend Cromer, came that afternoon.

While I was dreaming, or perhaps I was hallucinating, my church family had not forgotten me, but that day, when the minister visited, I understood how faithful they were in their prayers.

"Nick, I want to tell you something you don't know," said the pastor. "Three weeks after your surgery, I called Ann between Sunday school and church service to find out how you were doing. She told me she'd just asked the neurosurgeon how much longer you'd be in the coma. He told her he didn't know. 'Some patients remain in a coma for years.' He wasn't sure you'd ever recover."

Reverend Cromer said he completed the sermon and then did something he had never done in twelve years as a pastor. "I invited the deacons and the congregation who could comfortably kneel at the altar to come and pray for your recovery. After church, your good friend Bob Merck came up and asked me what I knew. 'Ann said it doesn't look promising,' I told him. 'She got no encouragement from the doctor.' Bob immediately said, 'I'm going to Duke.'"

I knew the rest of the story.

When Bob turned the doorknob, the metallic noise from the door mechanism brought me out of my deep coma. My eyes popped open. I talked with my friend four or five minutes before drifting into a semi-coma. There, markedly improved but still in peril, I would remain for those last five weeks. But even as I struggled through the valley of the shadow of death, good doctors, prayers, and a miracle worked together and saved my life.

You are also asking me
questions and I hear you,
I answer that I cannot answer,
you must find out for yourself.
Walt Whitman

Moving On

Each of us has the right and the responsibility to assess the roads which lie ahead, and those over which we have traveled, and if the future road looms ominous or unpromising, and the roads back uninviting, then we need to gather our resolve and, carrying only the necessary baggage, step off that road into another direction.

Maya Angelou

Three Generation Breakfast
S. Jane Gari

There's a file on my computer titled "Three Generation Breakfast." It contains a picture of me breastfeeding my five-day-old daughter while my mom spoon-feeds me eggs. At the time, my mom was nursing me back from the brink of severe post C-section anemia. In my sleep-deprived state of new motherhood, I assumed my uncontrollable shivering and mild hallucinating were par for the course, until the fifth morning home from the hospital. When I swung my legs over the side of the bed, I looked down to where my feet should be and saw only the carpet. My legs appeared to end at my ankles. I reached toward my missing feet in some desperate attempt to conjure them into being, only to discover my hands looked as tiny as my newborn's.

A thirst for reassurance outweighed the fear of being institutionalized, and I called my OB/GYN. She suspected low iron levels might be leaching all reliability from my already overtaxed nervous system. I was rooting for that diagnosis. Crazy was something I'd been called but didn't want to be.

My mom ushered me to the doctor and filled my prescriptions while I sat in the car and ate the tuna fish sandwich she'd made for me. The way she swooped into my home and took care of me while I was learning to take care of my new baby was a gift for which I had no adequate thank you. I wept from an overwhelming gratitude that made me feel as if I'd burst. Holding my daughter as she gripped my thumb with her impossibly small fingers; eating my mother's casseroles; being able to nap for a few hours at a clip—it was all so humbling, and the force of it reshaped my perspective—on *almost* everything.

I forgave so much about my mother in that first week I became a mother myself. And I asked for forgiveness in return. I apologized for not calling when my plane landed safely in England fourteen years earlier. I apologized for every time I came home late, for every time I'd ever worried her. Because now I understood some of what I'd previously thought were neuroses.

By no means did I understand everything about my mother, but I now had a glimpse of something. You lose a lot of your selfishness when you have a baby, or rather your selfishness is ripped from your body along with the tiny human who crawls out of you that day. It's as if the baby dislodges some part of you that's obsolete or can no longer be tolerated. That part is replaced by a new love that is more like a desperation, leaving you crazed and willing to tear out someone's arteries to save your child.

And this left me wondering if that was why my mom betrayed me. Her own desperation had run its course, and she was merely reclaiming some of the self I'd ripped from her. Maybe she said to herself, "My husband touched you. He acted inappropriately. But I still love him. You're an adult with your own life now. I will do nothing about this."

When I was nineteen, I told her about my stepfather's indiscretions. Her initial response was to scrawl shorthand versions of my account on a legal pad, as if preparing notes for the defense—not mine. I never dragged our family into court. Nothing could be proven. There had been no rape. My mother decided to settle the matter by believing that I believed my account. In this way, she could go on with her life as if nothing had happened and enable her own denial. By that time, I lived 800 miles away. We could see each other without my stepfather being involved. No life-altering arrangements necessary.

But imagining her inaction as an inglorious reclaiming of her selfhood still didn't help me. Her decision to take his side made me fear we might all be destined to become strangers to our parents and to our children—strangers with a shared history, but separate present and future tenses. It was a troubling dichotomy. I both understood and did not understand so much about her in the first week of my own motherhood. And that hasn't changed much. I look at my daughter, and know I would come to her defense. How could my own mother drop the ball so tragically?

When I was little, my mother was a giant who held in her hands the power to exalt or crush me. I guess it's that way with most people's parents. When I was four, she built me a dollhouse for Christmas. It quickly became an enduring symbol of her love and the extent to which she would go to express that devotion. I loved it and made sure it moved everywhere our family moved. And we moved a lot.

While I was finishing graduate school, I moved into a new apartment, the dollhouse in tow. Lugging my boxed-up life to the second-floor of a building without elevators wasn't fun. I started second-guessing the necessity of each box's contents.

"Do I really need this?" I asked myself after every haul up the stairs.

The dollhouse loomed alone in the back of the U-Haul. Getting it to the door of the building was easy. The U-Haul was equipped with a hand truck. The stairs were challenging, but they were carpeted and could operate like a ramp. All I had to do was lean the monolith against the edges of the steps and drag it up. So I did—all the way to the landing of the second floor.

The weight, that had so effortlessly traversed the staircase, teetered on the edge of the landing while I wrestled with the question. The one I had asked myself over and over again that afternoon.

"Do I really need this?"

And I decided I didn't. I didn't need the reminder of how wonderful she had once been when all I wanted was to grab her shoulders and scream at her for being too weak to show me how to be brave, for making me do it on my own.

I let go. I made her pay. I made both of us pay by breaking what we both had loved so much. I propped it up on the edge of the steps and pushed it. Gently. And then I watched it collapse and split open, fragments of the tiny home hurtling through the stairwell with all the force of a broken heart.

I regretted it instantly. I sobbed for both of us—a mother and daughter unable to come to an understanding of one another, unable to  talk about the past without dodging the landmines of open wounds. I wanted nothing to do with her husband. She wanted me to either forgive him in a way that involved acting like nothing had ever happened or to recant my accusations altogether. Many times over the years I considered doing just that. But I'm not a liar. I couldn't betray myself. Recanting would make her happy, but it would eat away at me for the rest of my life.

Neither one of us likes the other's stance on the issue, so we don't talk about it. But it's always there. The ice of this glacier has been melted and refrozen several times over by my foray into motherhood. On the one hand, my mother is a vault of advice and experience, and on the other, I have a hard time forgetting how she handled the information I had the guts to give her when I was nineteen.

I told her that her husband deliberately sought me out when I was alone, waited until I was asleep and fondled me. If this had been anyone else in the world, my mother would have executed vigilante

151

justice and happily sat in jail. But her husband? No. Perhaps two failed marriages were not an option. Perhaps she decided that because I was no longer an immediate presence in her life, she could afford the collateral damage of taking his side.

I handle grief by sorting through it and making a story. Words have long been a refuge for my secret thinking. Without them, I probably would have lost my purchase on sanity. I started writing about the whole ordeal with my mother and her husband several years ago, a few months after my daughter was born. The compulsion to write it all down was triggered by the love for my own daughter and playing what-if games in my head. How would I respond if my daughter ever came to me with something like the bomb I'd dropped on my mother?

I would muster the courage to be her champion, even if it meant scraping my ego bare. That thought continues to stop me. It makes me pull at all the old threads and try to understand why my own mother refused to do that for me.

And now there's

a memoir unpacking all of the causes and effects, the tantrums and solace. I had to do it—self-preservation drove the effort. My mother knows I wrote the book. She knows me so well, she guessed at it before I told her. And once again she's faced with a decision. My impressions of the past are laid out in black and white, without her spin, without her excuses. And she will either accept it or reject it. But no matter what she decides, I hope she will understand my act as vindication and not vindictiveness.

I love my mother; I always will. But love doesn't preclude rage. And pent-up rage has to find a way to retreat—otherwise there would be no holidays, no three-generation breakfast, no photograph to bear witness to the stubborn bonds of love strewn in the wake of an unresolvable past.

Come, Holy Hour
Lyrics, Paddy Bell

Come, holy hour,
I hear the whip-poor-will,
an overture
for my departing.

Trembling and frail,
dry russet blossoms fall,
surrender to
the heavy weight of time.

I must out-run
the dry dust of summer,
follow the path
of shadow and shade.

Settle to sleep
through colorless seasons.
Then I'll wake
to a spring serenade.

Come, holy hour,
I hear the whip-poor-will
Calm, holy hour,
magic hour.
Come, come, come, holy hour.

Moving On
Jayne Padgett Bowers

Counting Jimmy the realtor, six of us huddled together on the porch waiting for someone to let us in. Mrs. Sanders, petite and seventyish, opened the double front doors. With a sweeping gesture of her arm, she stepped back to welcome us into what would become our home for the next six years. Standing in the foyer, I took a quick look in all directions and said, "I think this is an answer to my prayers."

The lady of the house leaned in like a conspirator and touched my shoulder. "Honey," she said, "I know you're an answer to mine."

I liked her immediately.

The spacious house on Citadel Drive was all we'd dreamed about and more—four bedrooms and enough space for three kids and their parents to have some breathing room. There was even a screened-in back porch that stretched all the way across the back of the house and provided a view of Quail Creek Golf Course. Visions of wicker furniture danced in my head—a loveseat and at least two chairs. Naturally, there'd have to be a table for books, snacks, and beverages.

The living and dining rooms sat in the middle of the house with a giant fireplace dividing them. To the left of the foyer and living room, there was a hall with three bedrooms, two separated by a bookcase and built-in cabinets. Across the narrow hall was another bedroom, perfect for an active little boy. Located at the end of the passageway, the master bedroom overlooked the back porch. I nearly swooned when I saw the huge walk-in closet. *No more crammin' and jammin'.*

The short hall to the right of the foyer led to a family room, kitchen, and another dining area. A bar with a white-tiled countertop stood between the dining area and kitchen, and I wondered whether Hucks and Washington, my favorite furniture store in Conway, would have the perfect barstools. The previous owners had enclosed the attached garage and turned it into a second family room, complete with shelves and cabinets galore. *Would a pool table fit in there?*

I had to remind myself not to drool at the space and layout. What a house. It got better. The realtor strolled outside with us and pointed out the double car garage and a run-down tennis court. That's right. There was a tennis court on the property. There were tufts of grass poking through cracks in the surface, potholes galore, and areas of "pushed-up" asphalt. Still, it had promise.

"Maybe we could put a basketball goal here for the kids to practice," my husband said as he stood, arms crossed, watching the children as they scampered about the long-neglected court.

"Yeah, maybe," I said, playing it cool but inwardly elated that he was buying into the idea of owning this fabulous home.

The price was right, and a month later we moved in.

Six years later, we moved out. That morning, I woke up after a fitful night to the sound of a woodpecker tap, tap, tapping on one of the porch posts. Turns out it was my brother Mike rapping on my window to let me know he was outside and ready to help me move out of my dream house into a smaller home down the street. It was dark outside, not even six o'clock yet, and he had driven three hours from Columbia to lend some muscle and moral support.

"Let's eat breakfast somewhere in Conway before picking up the U-Haul," I suggested. "There's no way I'm going to unpack kitchen stuff to scramble eggs."

"Seriously, Sis? I thought you'd have quite the spread prepared. You know we're gonna need a lot of energy."

"Ha-ha. Huddle House has everything we need. Come on, let's go."

We caught up on family news over waffles and bacon and then went to pick up the moving van. I was excited about what I perceived to be an adventure and eager to get situated in the new house. Though a lot smaller, it had potential and sat on a pretty corner lot with a dozen pine trees.

The morning sun had shone down through the tall pines the day I first noticed the house, almost as though the luminous, golden rays were spotlighting the small, white ranch just for us.

"What do you think about that house, Paul?" I asked my son. Only thirteen, he'd be living with me longer than either of his sisters, and I wanted him to be happy, as happy as a child whose parents were separated could be.

"The one on the corner?"

"Yes."

"It's fine."

"Really? You like it? See the way the sun is shining on the roof? That's a message from above if I ever saw one."

Accustomed to his mother's sometimes off-the-wall comments, he replied in typical teen-aged fashion, "Yeah, it's okay."

I interpreted his "okay" to mean perfect and called the realtor to set up a time to see the property. My son and I looked at it that afternoon, and although it needed new flooring in all the rooms, fresh paint, and a few other updates, the house was solidly built and relatively new. I made an offer the next day, and by Thanksgiving, it was ours.

In the weeks to come, we replaced the flooring, painted the rooms, hung curtains, and did everything we could to make our new home uniquely ours. I let the children choose paint colors for their bathroom and bedrooms. Aiming for a coastal theme, they chose a bright, cool, turquoise for the bathroom. It was *Nautical*, a Lowe's color that brought a fun ambience to the center of the house.

***

The new owners of our house down the block, the one with the screened-in porch and colossal walk-in closet, were scheduled to take possession the Saturday after Thanksgiving, and we planned to finish the moving process on Friday. One of my daughters was already living in an apartment with friends, and the other one was working most of the day, thus leaving the bulk of the moving to their brother, uncle, and mother.

We worked like Trojans all day. At first the packing was orderly and methodical, but as the morning progressed, things went from organized to chaotic, from neat to sloppy. We soon tired of labeling boxes and just threw them pell-mell into the truck. Instead of carefully considering each belonging's final destination, we crammed possessions into Hefty bags earmarked for donation.

After dumping off the boxes at my new house and helping me set up three beds, Mike and I made a run into Conway to deliver bags to Salvation Army and turn in the U-Haul. As quickly as he had appeared early that morning, he disappeared late that afternoon, leaving me amidst boxes, bags, and furniture placed haphazardly throughout the house.

Paul soon left to spend what was left of the weekend with his father. I was alone, unexpectedly caught off guard at the eeriness of the situation. I looked around at the disordered clutter and felt the urge to go back to the Citadel Drive home for a final walkthrough. I grabbed my house keys and walked the two blocks to what had once been my dream house.

Every light in the house was on, and there were three cars in the driveway and one in the circular drive. The new owners were to take possession Saturday, and this was Friday evening. A little baffled by what was happening, I pushed open the sliding glass door on the back porch and stepped into the eating area.

It was a surreal scene. I was there, but no one appeared to notice. *Am I dreaming?*

Three women were in the kitchen busily preparing food for an after-Thanksgiving meal. *What were they doing in my kitchen? Who were these strangers who didn't even notice me—the woman who had scrubbed the floors, chosen paint colors, and sat with her family around a table in that very space for the past six years?* They'd probably think it was tacky to keep an antique bowl of golf balls in the center of the table.

There was the counter where my father had sat watching my young son fry bologna for their breakfast one morning. I glanced across the family room rapidly filling up with *their* furniture and stared at an empty corner, recalling that I had repositioned a table in that spot after my mother's tactful suggestion that I place it catty-cornered. Since I seemed to be invisible to the worker bees, I continued my farewell tour.

Crossing the threshold to the dining room, I remembered darting through there one afternoon and seeing Elizabeth, my younger daughter, diligently doing her homework. She had looked up at me with a sweet smile, and although I knew her writing was likely to leave tiny indentations on the brand new mahogany table, I let it pass, later suggesting that she always put some sort of cushion between her work and the table.

Lingering in the dining room a few seconds longer, I recalled the Thanksgiving when both sides of the family had come for the feast. We'd extended the dining space onto the back porch and left the dining room door open to catch the cheery voices and jolly laughter wafting back and forth. My brother Mike and his wife had brought a young Chinese couple with them from Columbia. Their baby's black hair stuck out in spikes all around his precious head.

I took a deep breath and walked towards the bedrooms, annoyed that the new owners had decided to move in a day early. The men were in the bedrooms setting up box springs and mattresses. To my surprise, they'd chosen a different wall for the headboard in the master bedroom, and there was now a doggie bed in the room where I'd slept the night before.

I couldn't bear to see my children's rooms rearranged so I strolled back towards the foyer and peeked out into the night, the circular drive brightened by the glow of the front porch light. We had surprised my oldest daughter with her first car in that circle one sunny August morning. She was sixteen, and the car was a used, celery-green Chevy compact that had been dubbed the *Benmobile* by its previous owner.

I meandered into the kitchen and found the new woman of the house going through cabinets. I walked over to give her my only remaining key and told her I hoped she'd enjoy the house as much as we had. Barely acknowledging my presence, she pointed to some glassware, plates and small cups, and asked, "Do you want these?"

"No," I said, shrugging. "I've never used them. They belonged to the woman who lived here before I did. Guess I figured she'd come back for them sooner or later."

"Well, I don't have room for them," she replied and went back to arranging dishes in *her* cabinets.

I reached into my jeans pocket for the key, and without saying another word, I placed it on the shiny white-tiled counter. Quietly and unnoticed, I left the way I had come.

Mom's Big Move for Us

Brenda Bevan Remmes (as told to her by her husband Bill)

At the beginning of my brother John's senior year in 1961, Mom came up with a plan. She started talking to us about college. She couldn't afford to pay the tuition but she promised that she would move to any place we wanted that had a university. She would get a job and provide us with room and board. We, in turn, could find jobs in order to pay the tuition. John got his choice. He picked The University of Iowa in Iowa City.

When I look back at her offer at this time in her life, I am amazed. She was a fifty-one-year-old widow who had rarely been more than twenty miles away from her parents. Mom knew no one in Iowa City. She didn't own or drive a car, but she believed in herself enough to take the risks. She wanted her boys to have more choices than Denison offered.

Sisakmilar to his reaction when she wanted to get married, Grandpa Laubscher adamantly opposed the idea of her leaving Denison. When she asked for a loan, he refused. Without any encouragement or support, Mom boarded a bus on her own and headed 220 miles east on a five-hour trip to find a job.

Her first stop was the Veterans Administration Hospital. By all rights she would have qualified for a job there, but she'd never taken a standardized test. They handed her one. She got flustered. She fumbled over the words and got confused by the pictures. If she had been given an oral test or asked to demonstrate how to use certain equipment she would have passed, but when required to read and write her answers— she failed.

She persisted. Her next stop was The University of Iowa Hospital where no test was required for her to secure a job as a diet maid in the nutrition department. She'd be responsible for delivering meals to patients. Grandpa caved in once he realized Mom had a job and planned to leave with or without his blessings. He provided a farm truck to help us carry our furniture from one side of the state to the other.

Mom calculated her projected income and found a three-bedroom duplex for $215 per month which she could afford if she rented out one of the rooms to another student. That began the next round of us having other people living with us.

To her distress, the first boarder didn't work out too well. Mom thought she'd prefer to have a female student in the spare bedroom, but the young lady who moved in took an immediate shine to John, which didn't surprise me in the least. Mom had her out within the week.

Until now, Mom had never had trouble writing checks in Denison, but when she got to Iowa City she was required to have a driver's license as ID. So at fifty-one she set out to get a driver's license. John and I tried to teach her to drive, but she was a nervous driver and chose to let us take her anywhere that she couldn't walk or catch a bus. She only wanted the identification. She never intended to drive. She passed the test and got the ID.

When home on leave that year, Betty offered to take Mom to see the and John and I encouraged her to let Mom drive once she got out on some of those lonely stretches in Nebraska. "She needs some driving experience," we insisted.

Betty talks about Mom's brief time behind the wheel with laughter. "She was driving about 20 miles an hour and whenever we'd come to a stop sign, she'd slam on the brakes sending us both jolting into the dashboard. Nobody had seatbelts back then.

"'Mom,' I'd say, 'you gotta drive faster or we'll never get there, and when you come to a stop, don't hit the brakes so hard—stop gradually.'

"It wasn't too many more miles when she told me she didn't want to drive anymore because I was making her nervous. I told her to pull over to the side, which she did—right into a row of mailboxes by the road. A farmer came out of his house and walked down to the road to help us pull one mailbox out from under the car. When we got back in the car she was disgusted with me."

"*See what you did,* she said. '*I drove fast—like you told me—and I didn't slam on the brakes when I needed to stop, like you told me and look what happened.*

"When we finally got to the Grand Canyon, she took one look and said, *It's just a big ditch. No way to plant a crop in there. Let's go home.*"

Neighbor Lady
Laura Bruno Lilly

Neighbor Lady
Kinda cranky.
Just old.
That's all.
Just old.
Always out
Weeding weeds
Raking leaves.
Tending things.
Neighbor Lady
Springtime's here.
Your garden hat
and gloves and things
are piled high
in garbage cans.
Dandelions sprout
Too fast too soon.
Empty house.
For sale sign.
Neighbor Lady
Kinda cranky.
Too old.
That's all.
Too old.

All's Well
Douglas Wyant

My cell phone wakes me at 10:48 p.m., Monday, August 15. The screen identifies the caller as Jonathan.

I wonder, *Is anything wrong?*

My oldest son lives in Murfreesboro, Tennessee, with his wife Claire and their son Camden, who arrived at 1:02 a.m., Sunday, July 31, 2016, five weeks early.

"Hello."

No response.

"Jonathan?"

A week before Camden's early arrival, Jonathan and Claire signed documents to purchase a three-bedroom house in the suburbs. As I listen to him hum to himself, I visualize Jonathan puttering around in the old house on Lytle Street, packing belongings to move to their new house across town, and I realize he has made a *butt call.*

In an instant, I am transported back to our house in Kirkover Hills forty-two years ago. From the master bedroom, I hear Jonathan burble in his crib on the baby monitor in the nursery.

I smile at the memory. At this hour, all's well. I end the call and drift off to sleep.

I'm Crazy
Martha Dabbs Greenway

I'm crazy about the South
    love the softer tones of speech
    slower pace of life
the salty taste of boiled peanuts.

I'm crazy about the South
    barbecue only on weekends
    bountiful bourbon
those buttery biscuits, comfort to my soul.

I'm crazy about the South
    lovable characters
    slightly lazy language
the hazy mornings of high humidity.

I'm crazy about the South
    symphony of tree frogs after a rain
    hoots of a lonesome Barred Owl at night
the howl of hounds on a hunting weekend.

I'm crazy about the South, but
    I've never lived anywhere else.
    I've only visited, knowing
I'd return home.

Seaside Reflections
Jayne Padgett Bowers

I left the beach reluctantly on Labor Day, turning at the top of the boardwalk steps for one last sweeping glance. How many times had I seen this same stretch of sand and surf? Life was slipping away far too quickly, and I knew I'd miss the:

Splat of wet sand as I walked by the edge of the sea
Splashes of the ocean tickling my ankles
Slap of my Rainbow flip-flops against my soles
Squealing of ecstatic kids
Squishiness of soft, wet sand
Scrunching of tiny shells being drenched in salt water
Shimmering sun on the ocean in early morning
Skittering sanderlings scooting about their business
Swashes filled with rushing water
Sheltering shade beneath the piers

For years, I lived near the ocean and could feel its mighty power from as many as fifteen miles away. A co-worker always kept a beach chair in the car just in case she had twenty or thirty minutes to replenish her soul. Although my circumstances didn't allow such spontaneity, I could get still and imagine the silent, hunkering seabirds as they stood at allegiance beside the ocean and feel peace.

A student once gave me a card with a seascape on the front, a red wooden chair perched on a sand dune and wild birds swooping around and above the empty chair. I framed the card and hung it in my office to look at when stressed or tired. *There's my chair. It's waiting for me*, I'd think. I still have the framed card, but I don't know where the student is or what happened to her. Life moved on for both of us.

On this beach, I was a teen who slathered baby oil and Coppertone on my skin and soaked up the sun with friends while giggling and talking about—what else? Boys, parents, teachers, curfews, and the weekend's activities. So focused were we on living in the moment, future plans and long range goals rarely cropped up in our conversations.

Later, as a young adult who had put things of childhood behind, I was completely ignorant about everything that lay ahead. I was still a spring chicken, filled with book knowledge but low on experience. I'd sit on the beach with friends discussing love, marriage, and the baby carriage versus the advantages of establishing a career. For the first time since Rosie the Riveter went back to the kitchen, American women were reentering the workforce.

Fast forward a few years, and I was the young mother who stood at the edge of the water, ever vigilant lest one of the children stumble or venture too far into the ocean. "Come back, come back.

You're in too deep," was my constant refrain. *You just don't know how treacherous the ocean is,* I'd think, little realizing those protective words symbolized other warnings

Life has its seasons. Long past the summer of my life, I am entering late fall, also a season of delight and pleasure. I'm the grandmother who walks the beach, mostly alone, remembering earlier days and pondering the layers of meanings in beach terms:

Raging seas where a person could drown without support
Stinging jellyfish that look deceptively harmless
Stormy weather that could throw someone off course
Shifting sands that mimic the transient days of our lives

Monsters in the deep that can bite and pull a person under
Winds that force a change of direction

I've learned that despite the sea monsters and stormy weather, the sun always rises the next day. Even the most opacus clouds can't obscure its brilliance for long.

Once our family went through a period of taking turns choosing a quote of the week to share with the one another. The written phrase was stuck on the front of the refrigerator for all to see and ponder. One morning before school I recall being a bit bothered by my sixteen-year-old son's quote: "No matter how dark the night, morning always comes."

What kind of darkness could my child possibly be experiencing that I didn't know about? About that time, he whizzed into the kitchen and opened the fridge for some orange juice. He looked fine, no dark circles under his eyes or sad expression.

"What's up with that quote, Bud?" I asked, deciding that a straightforward approach was best.

"You like it?" he asked, swigging some orange juice right from the container and looking quite pleased with himself.

"Not sure. Just trying to figure out what it means to you and why you chose it."

"Oh, it's from a video game. I like it, that's all."

"A video game?" I asked, relieved.

"Yeah, *Final Fantasy X*," he answered, his blue-eyed gaze steady and convincing.

***

All lives change. It's just the details that differ. I once worked with a man who disliked teaching Human Growth and Development because, in his words, "People grow up, grow old, and die." Ever the cynic, he was deaf to colleagues' insistence on life's mysteries and magic.

People fall in love, marry, divorce, remarry, stay single, cohabitate, drop out of school, graduate from college, join the military, buy homes, have children, move to California, join the working world, move out of their parents' home, move back into their parents' home as part of the Boomerang Generation, dress for success, establish careers, bury loved ones, retire, buy a house at the lake, eat tofu, hike the Appalachian Trail, travel, practice yoga, and search for meaning. *What am I doing here and where am I going?*

Children go from growing beneath their mother's heart to starting to school. In a flash, the parent turns around and sees her adult offspring raising children of their own, and if they want advice, they'll ask, *thank you very much*. You want them to be independent and responsible adults. But you want them to stay your children, too. Kahlil Gibran's reminder from "On Children" that our children are not really our children haunts many parents, me included. Parents might house their bodies, Gibran says, but not their souls,

> For their souls dwell in the house of tomorrow,
> Which you cannot visit, not even in your dreams.

Of all the mysteries, death is the most profound. My husband lost a beloved son to cancer. Many friends and acquaintances lose their children to disease, accident, war, suicide, and drug overdose. Sometimes the passing is sudden and unexpected with no time to say goodbye. Other times, death comes after a lingering illness. No matter the circumstance, the cut is deep and permanent. Bonnie Raitt assures us that time *ain't never healed a wound* and asks, "Can you think of anything that gets any better because it's old?" *Not really, Bonnie. No.*

One evening, my daughter and I visited a church member, a spunky, gray-haired woman in her late seventies, and as we sat on her comfortable sofa learning more about her reasons for moving to the coast, I heard her mention a son. I knew she had a daughter who lived in a distant state but was unaware of another child. Assuming that there was some dark drama behind her reason for not sharing this fact, I said nothing.

"He would have been fifty-three this month," she said, looking down at her clasped hands.

"I didn't know you had another child," I replied.

"He was our first. Lucinda came along two years later."

Sensing that she wanted to talk about it, curiosity and concern prompted me to ask, "What happened to your son? Was he a little boy when he passed away?"

"He was a wee little thing, only three, always running around getting into mischief."

I waited, wondering if he had died of scarlet fever or some other malady that medical science had been unable to treat in earlier years.

Turning towards Carrie and me, she said, "He fell from a second-story window and died on impact."

The horror of it all struck me with such force that I gasped and said, "Oh Lillie, how did you ever get over that?"

"I never have," she said, shaking her head.

Here she was in the winter of her life, still grieving a child who had died in a tragic accident fifty years prior. Like so many walking wounded, she carried his memory in her heart, even imagining what he'd have been like at fifty-three. I knew instinctively that Lillie had visualized her son at all ages.

Some people lose their parents early on. A classmate's mother passed away when my friend was seven, leaving a grieving widower to raise his two young daughters. Others have parents who live well into their nineties. Moving away from my hometown helped assuage the death of my parents since we incrementally moved away from one another in physical and emotional ways over the decades.

Still, there are moments when I think, *I'll ask Mama*. And then I remember. If someone teases me about what they perceive to be a far out idea, I'll look heavenward and wonder, *Did you hear that, Daddy?* Open to ideas beyond those of his provincial upbringing, he understood my search for truth.

Everyone experiences moments too splendid for words and some too painful to recall. We get our hearts broken. We feel love and acceptance and suffer disappointment and heartache, yet this sweet old world keeps turning on its axis. We press on towards the winter, bracing for the cold temperatures and barren landscapes, hoping to call on the reserves of strength built from our earlier experiences.

At the same time, there's nothing wrong with keeping a little summer in one's life, regardless of the season. Tonight I'll be flip-flopping around in my Rainbows and recalling days spent in the summer and fall of my life. There was sunshine, lots of it, and wind and rain, too.

A Listener's Lament
Douglas Wyant

I like country music.
Classic country music.
Songs that tell a story.
Songs that bring tears to my eyes:
"I Can't Stop Loving You..."
"He Stopped Loving Her Today."

Most contemporary country music
is all thunder and lightning,
no rain.

The Road Ahead

What we call the beginning is
often the end
And to make our end is to make a
Beginning.
The end is where we start from.
                    T.S. Eliot

183

The Flight
Myra Yeatts

My flight from Columbia to Grand Rapids started at 7 a.m. I had become a seasoned traveler in previous months since my sister's illness. Now in her last days, there was still so much to say.

I boarded the plane and delighted in my seat location behind first class. Actual leg room. I pulled out a novel to look occupied, so as not to be drawn into a tedious conversation with the person who would sit beside me. These small crafts always filled up.

"Wow, this is a great seat," said the slender young man stowing his carry-on in the overhead. He grinned rakishly. I moved my purse to the other side of me, then decided to stuff it deeply into the pocket in front of me and keep my eye on it.

"Grand Rapids your final destination, or are you connecting there?" he asked as he settled himself and stretched out his long, jean-clad legs.

"Final destination." With short answers, the conversation usually lapsed, and I didn't want to talk. I wanted to hide in my book, turn the pages once in a while and think.

"You got family there?"

"Yes."

"Children, grandchildren?"

Well, this wasn't working. I had a talker on my hands. I took a deep breath and was about to tell him I needed to meditate or something, but his sincere face revealed someone eager for communication. "My sister and her children and grandchildren."

"I'm visiting some friends in a little town thirty miles from Grand Rapids. Just got back from Pakistan. Man, it's good to be stateside."

He would have gone on, but my cell phone rang. I checked the ID. It was Elaine, my sister's daughter. Just as I said hello, the pilot came on the crackling intercom to announce the weather conditions and the length of our flight.

"Say again, Elaine. I couldn't hear you."

"Mom died a few minutes ago. We wanted to let you know in case you didn't want to make the flight."

Then all the other announcements started and the plane began to move. I knew I had to shut off my phone.

"I'm coming, Elaine," I said and disconnected. I crumbled back into the seat and muttered through tears, "Too late. I've lost her."

"Sorry, did you say something?"

"Janice…my sister died. I didn't get there in time."

"That's really tough. I'm so sorry for your loss." He clumsily patted my knee. "My mom died of multiple sclerosis during my last tour. It's hard to grieve among strangers." He continued talking softly as our plane lifted into the steel-colored sky. "People say they're sorry,

185

but they're really sorry they got caught in the wrong place at the wrong time and have to say they're sorry." The irony bit into both of us, and we smiled at each other.

When the seatbelt light went off, he turned in his seat so that his back faced the aisle and crossed his arms over his soft blue sweater that matched his eyes. He settled in for a long intimate conversation. "So tell me about her."

His patient gentleness pulled conversation from me. "So full of life. She was a bank manager, president of her garden club and book club. She conducted sight-seeing tours in Holland, Michigan, during the Tulip Festival. You would have liked her. Everyone did. She was the social director for the senior citizen community center after she retired from banking. She…"

"That's what she did. Who was she to you?"

I pulled out another Kleenex while choking back fresh tears, but conceded that I needed to talk about her. "She was as much a mother as a sister. She took me in as a surly teenager and made me toe the line. I figured out pretty quick I couldn't pull anything on her. She was savvy to game-playing. Even though I complained loudly, having someone who understood me and still cared helped me through those brutal teenage years. I seldom made a move without consulting her. Even recently. She was my advisor, my cheerleader, and always my best friend."

"Sounds like my mom."

He began to tell me about his mother and their trials with his adolescent behavior, her heroic light-hearted attitude about her disease, and her swift justice with his rebellious nature. He engaged me so completely with his outlandish stories, laughter bubbled up. Then I suddenly felt like a traitor.

He smiled his charming smile and patted me on the knee again. Not quite so clumsily. He seemed to read my mind. "It's okay. You need to live and live bigger now…for her and you."

"I won't know what to do without my coach."

He fingered a chain around his neck and pulled out a small silver cross. "I noticed you wear one of these." He brought his face within inches of mine and looked directly into my eyes. "You have a coach."

A bell dinged and the seat belt light came on. I dried my eyes and blew my nose. Pulling in a deep breath of stale plane air, I took a small mirror from my purse. My face must show strength to support my grieving family.

When the plane landed, I struggled getting my carry-on out of the overhead and pulling the handle out. I needed to get the young man's name. I turned to ask him if he had a card with an address, so I could thank him properly. He wasn't there.

Quickly reaching the steps, I searched the stretch of tarmac between the plane and the gate. It had been only a minute. Where was he? He was tall. I should be able to see his head. No trace of the blue sweater either. Impossible…but he was gone.

Ashes to Ashes
Douglas Wyant

Whenever we get together,
most often at funerals these days,
we stir up the embers of our memories
and sparks swirl up into the somber sky.

The Road Ahead
Jayne Padgett Bowers

Barely conscious, I didn't recognize the persistent *buzz buzz buzz* of my cell phone right away.

It was pitch-black outside. *Who would call at this hour?*

"Hello?" I mumbled.

"Hey, Sis. We're at the hospital with Daddy, and if you want to see him alive, you need to come now," my brother Mike said.

"What? Wait. I didn't even know he'd gotten worse," I said. "Why didn't someone tell me?"

"Just get here as quick as you can," he said. All business.

"So it's serious?" I asked, realizing the silliness of the question, yet too muddled to say anything else.

"Like I said," Mike replied before breaking the connection.

I jumped out of bed and quickly crossed the hall to my daughter Carrie's room. Cracking open the door, I said, "Sweetie, I hate to wake you up, but Daddy's in the hospital, and Uncle Mike says I need to come to Camden right now."

"Now? What time is it?" she asked, her dark hair a tousled cloud around her sleepy face.

"Around five. I'm taking a quick shower and hitting the road. I want you to come with me."

Twenty-five minutes later, we pulled out of the driveway, tired and yet strangely alert. Minds racing with what lay before us, we rode through the predawn October morning silently noting familiar sights. There was Coastal Carolina, streetlights glowing along the still quiet avenues where sleeping students perhaps dreamed of love, laughter, and happily ever after. Lucky them.

We stopped at the intersection of University Boulevard and Highway 544. Hillcrest Cemetery stared us square in the face. I had attended numerous graveside services at Hillcrest and even considered being buried there at some point in the distant future. Having traveled that stretch of Highway 544 thousands of times, I associated the area with life and energy. *It might be nice to have a final resting place in the hub of so much coming and going,* I thought.

That morning, however, the shadowy shapes of tombstones and trees filled me with dread and apprehension. Would I be standing in another such location 115 miles away before the week's end? I squelched the thought and turned right towards Conway and Highway 501, the thoroughfare to Florence.

Stopped by the traffic light at the intersection of Church Street and Ninth Avenue in Conway, we glanced at the surrounding restaurants, El Cerro on the left and Pizza Hut and Wendy's on the right. Dark and quiet, they'd all be buzzing with the after-church crowd in a few hours.

Gazing down Ninth Avenue, Carrie asked, "Do you remember that morning we had a little fender bender on the way to school?"

I did indeed. It was the same day I'd later attended the funeral of a student killed in a car accident. Rushing to get the children to their separate schools had been especially challenging that morning.

Waiting for the light to change, I recalled the one and only time my father took me to school. We lived only two blocks away, so most of the time I walked with other kids, a gaggle of us laughing and talking and kicking up leaves.

But I felt like big stuff that winter's day.

My father took me to school in his truck, and I sat up high and happy on the passenger side. Sneaking a glance at him, I thought he looked like a movie star, cigarette held between his middle and forefinger, both of us clueless that the smoke had already begun its dirty work.

Proud that such a cool man was my father, I asked, "How old are you, Daddy?"

"Twenty-six."

That old? Momentarily shocked at his advanced age, I tried to bolster his confidence and assure him that he had many years ahead of him despite his approaching dotage. "That's not so old." I replied.

He didn't say anything. Just gave me an amused look that, in retrospect, said, *Are you for real?*

He pulled up to the playground, and we both gazed at the running, jumping, skipping kids just beyond the fence. Leaning over to give me a quick kiss on the cheek, he said, "Be a good girl."

"Okay, Daddy. See you tonight," I jumped down out of the truck and hurried towards my friends, second graders playing tag and hopscotch.

Years passed, and suddenly I was a young teenager, fifteen. A cute boy moved to town and invited my friends and me to a party at his house. *Everybody* would be there. What I didn't count on was my mother's adamant, "NO." She didn't know this family or whether the parents would actually be at the party, and no matter what strategy I used, I couldn't wear her down.

Two of my clever friends hatched a plan. We'd have a sleepover and leave from Becky's house. That plan worked so wonderfully well that I began to feel uneasy. Surely I'd be found out, and I didn't want to face my parents' disappointment.

As fate would have it, my mother phoned Becky's house to remind me of something, and Becky's mother spilled the beans. Hurt and angry, my mother called me at the cute new kid's home to let me know that my father was on the way to pick me up. I wasn't afraid, just ashamed that I'd been deliberately deceitful.

My two chums and I waited out front, and my father soon came cruising up in the family car, a silver '57 Chevy station wagon. I got in the front seat and glimpsed at his profile, his wavy black hair falling a little on to his forehead. That night I was again riding shotgun with my father, but this time the mood was somber. I was a blossoming teen, not a happy-go-lucky seven-year-old.

"Hey Daddy. I'm glad you came to pick us up," I said. Not the kind of teen to stray too far, I was suddenly grateful to have parents who cared enough to rein me in even if it meant coming out to a stranger's house to take me home. Parents at nineteen, they relied on love, common sense, and a trial-and-error approach to raise four

children. I doubt if they'd heard of B.F. Skinner or whether they'd pay much heed to his reinforcement theory if they had.

My father didn't reply, just inhaled and exhaled that cigarette smoke. My heart sank.

All the way from Lugoff, my friends implored him to please please please let me spend the night with them. Aware that he wasn't a man who could easily be swayed, I knew their entreaties were falling on deaf ears, and after a few minutes, we rode along in silence. After dropping them off, we went home. Home.

My father said, "Go sit down at the kitchen table. I'll be there in a minute." I sat at the table and watched my mother's back as she washed the dinner dishes. The table, rectangular with chrome legs and a yellow Formica top, was surrounded by six chairs with vinyl seats and backs that matched the tabletop.

Daddy came into the room and set a typewriter on the table, a gray Royal with white keys, and asked me if I knew what maxim meant.

"No, sir," I said, watching as he carefully rolled a sheet of paper into the typewriter.

He pushed the dictionary towards me and began to type several maxims and proverbs, all having to do with honesty, parental love, and morals. Head down and poised over the dictionary, I pretended a sincere and focused interest in its contents. The sound of typewriter keys striking the page was the only sound in the room.

After the longest ten minutes of my young life, Daddy removed the paper from the Royal and gave it a brief once-over. Satisfied with the quotes, he handed me the completed list with instructions to read and memorize it. I took the sheet of paper, thinking that now I could escape to the bedroom and away from his scrutiny. I was wrong.

My father then gave me an object lesson I've never forgotten.

"See your mother's dishpan? Imagine it's overflowing with money. Can you see that?"

"Yes, sir." *Would this night ever end?*

"I know you, and I know you'd never take anything that wasn't yours. But then one day you decide you want some bubble gum, so you take a penny. One little penny—you figure that won't hurt anyone. And no one will ever know the difference. So you steal the money and get the gum. It tastes sweet and chewy, and no one ever finds out. The next time you get a hankering for gum, you get more money. Then it's candy you want, some chocolate. Before you know it, you're taking dollar bills from the bottom."

"I'd never do that," I said.

"You wouldn't now. But it's a slippery slope, Honey. Whether you're stealing money for gum or deceiving your mother and me, it's dishonest."

Those words took up residence in my mind that night and never left. So many life lessons ran through my consciousness as I drove through the small towns of Aynor and Rains, aware of the speed limit but pushing it to the max.

A few months earlier, my father, unbeknownst to us, had been eavesdropping on a conversation Mike and I were having. Sitting in his tan leather recliner with the paper held up before his face, Daddy was deep into the editorials. We assumed our chatter was background noise until he put the paper on his lap and answered Mike's question about which one of us had given our parents the most grief.

"I know I was a rascal at times. I must have really tried your souls," my brother said, grinning, confident of his niche as rebel.

"No, actually it was Jayne," Daddy answered without a moment's hesitation.

"What?" we both asked.

"It was probably because she was the oldest, and we just didn't know what to do when she started doing what she wanted to do and not what we wanted her to do."

Mike and I stared at him, incredulous at this revelation.

He continued, "When you were little kids, your mother and I knew what to do, but when you hit the teen years, we fumbled a lot."

Daddy resumed his paper perusal, leaving Mike and me too stunned to say a word.

I had to get to Camden. I had to tell him I was sorry for being so defiant. I had to tell him that despite the rocky teen years, Mike and I had morphed into responsible adults because of his and Mama's firm guidance and many sacrifices.

Stopping outside of Florence at what used to be called Jimmy Carter's to fill up with gas, I placed the pump handle in the tank and called the hospital room for an update. My sister Ann answered on the first ring.

"We're on our way," I told her.

"Sorry, Sis. It's too late, he's gone," Ann said, her tone clipped and straightforward.

"What? Gone? What does that mean? He's...?"

"About five minutes ago. Mike was shaving him, and Allen was holding his head straight. They felt his head drop and knew something had changed."

"Can't believe it," I said, more to myself than to Ann.

"Mike finished the job."

"What job?"

"The shaving. Mama asked them to do it."

"Poor Mama," I said. "How is she?"

"Not sure. She was in the hall when it happened, and Mike just told her."

Leaning against the car, I imagined the sights and sounds in the room where my father's strong spirit had slipped away from his frail body, weakened by decades of smoking and the debilitating effects of emphysema. The steady, comforting *beep beep beep* of the heart monitor was now silent. My sister, one brother, their spouses, two aunts, and my mother were all clustered near the bed, the room quiet except for muffled cries and mumblings.

I should have been there. Why didn't someone call me earlier?

"How close are you?" Ann asked.

"We're almost to Florence. Can't talk anymore. Bye."

Dazed, I ended the call, put the pump handle back in its proper place, and got back in the car with Carrie. Sitting there, I tried to wrap my mind around the events that had taken place seventy miles down the road while I'd been speeding through the darkness.

"What's the matter, Mama? What did Aunt Ann say?"

"She said…she said Daddy died just a few minutes ago."

"Oh, Mama, I'm so sorry."

"I know, I know. It's too much to take in right now. I wish we could have been there. I wish someone had told me earlier. I wish, I wish, I wish."

"He's been in the hospital off and on for the past six months. They probably figured this was just another visit."

197

"Kind of like that story I used to tell you about the boy who cried wolf?"

"Something like that. Want me to drive?" she offered.

I looked at Carrie's pretty young face, tear-stained and weary, and realized the magnitude of the moment. "You really want to? I mean, do you feel like it?"

"Yes, ma'am," she said. We switched positions, Carrie in the driver's seat with me as her passenger. I buckled my seat belt and sank into the seat as my daughter smoothly maneuvered the Cutlass back onto the highway, headlights penetrating the inky sky.

I looked down the road ahead. It was so dark.

A Trip to Heaven
Paddy Bell

My mother was born in 1923 on December 12, the feast day of the patroness of Mexico, Our Lady of Guadalupe. A chalk statue of this Mexican Mary held a place of prominence in her home. It was vividly painted with intense, exotic, piñata-like colors with carvings of delicate pink roses at the base. She often placed a vase of fresh roses and greenery next to the statue, a reminder of the legend of the apparition of Our Lady and the roses that appeared miraculously on a Mexican mountaintop in the middle of winter.

Several months before her death, Mom lovingly carried that statue with her as she agreed to move in with me, my husband, and our little mixed-breed dog, Sadie. The sheepdog part of Sadie's mix kept her on high alert at Mom's side watching, comforting, as the two of them cuddled up in the hospital bed. I did everything possible to camouflage the fact of that bed, with sheets and quilts of playful design and soft brushed cotton coverlets draped over the unfriendly steel rails. Sadie's pillowy fur softened the situation further. Vases of Our Lady roses and gardenias scented the room, waging battle with the sensual assaults of time and mortality.

Our Lady of Guadalupe

As Mom's condition deteriorated, I slept in a separate bed in the room with her and Sadie. One particular night I was awakened by Sadie's' muted whimper and Mom's little voice.

"Oh, it's beautiful. Just beautiful."

"You okay? Are you awake?" I asked.

"It's more crowded than I thought it would be, Honey, but it's still quite roomy. Lots of room, really, room for many more."

I quieted the usual urge to dash to her side, content to let her sleep and dream undisturbed.

"More trees are needed," she said. Although her voice was faint, it was clear and confident. "Over there is space. That's right. And even more. We need them for the stars. Stars for the trees, trees for the stars. Then the brightest one of all in its place in the sky. There, for all to see. Listen! It's the angels."

Sadie raised her head, twitched her ears as she looked at me as if to assess my level of concern and to question my lack of action. Something was different in Mom's voice—an absence of anxiety. I hesitated, uncertain, and then she continued.

"Paddy," she said clearly, "you are the angel in charge of the others. Lead them in singing. Glory to the newborn king, the newborn king, the baby king."

Now identified in her dream, I listened even more intently, a captivated eavesdropping voyeur straining to catch every word. With pillows propped behind my head I gazed at her, praying for more. She did not disappoint.

"My favorite part!" she nearly squealed with joy. Sadie raised her head again and mewed an uneasy whine as Mom said, "The humble shepherds and all the sheep, wearing their shaggy winter coats, are gathered on the hill. Danny, can you count them—the sheep and the shepherds?"

Here I distinctly detected a small giggle. Somehow in her dream she made a little joke about counting sheep. I sensed her excitement and joy, and knew if she could, she would be clapping her hands in delight.

"How many? They've all come to see the infant. Oh, I'm so glad to be here, here on this special night. So special...."

Her voice trailed off and she fell silent. Sadie relaxed, laid her head on the pillow next to Mom. The crystal hummingbird nightlight cast just enough of a blush to see my mother—tiny and frail as a bird, under her bird-themed coverlet—birds in happy places, nests, perched on flowering branches, in pairs, all contentedly grounded, not in uncertain flight, but settled and restful—just like Mom and Sadie.

Minutes passed. I became anxious, fearful, as her breathing grew sluggish, too casual. I didn't want the story to be over, didn't want to disturb her sleep, but it seemed time for me to go to her. And then:

"There's a lantern far off. It seems to be floating in the darkness. Oh, it's the three Magi and the camel-tender is leading them with his lantern. I knew they would come, bringing gifts for the sleeping baby."

She paused, struggling with something.

"Dad! Hey, Dad! Why can't you hear me?"

The "Dad" she was calling was not her father, but mine. Since he'd passed away four years before, I knew that Mom's dreams and waking thoughts were of him, of their sixty-three years together, of their infinite love, and of her longing to be with him again.

"Do you see me?" she sighed, a catch in her breath, and tenuously asked, "Why can't you hear me? I'm here, Sweetie, I'm here." Again, her voice faded.

I desperately wondered what she was seeing. Where was this dream taking place? Was she really seeing my dad?

She and Sadie fell into unison with soft rhythmic sleeping sounds. I tried to take stock, to process her words, imagine the visions. I wondered where and what the dream was—or was not.

"Dad!"

I startled at the sudden energy and intensity of her voice and the speck of agitation as she called his name again.

"Time is getting closer and there's still much to do." Her words were filled with urgency. "That tree must be moved over there. More stars. They're so beautiful. Oh, my goodness, make sure that the children are down in the front. Yes, children, go close, close to the manger."

She paused, and in a faint tremulous quaver came the unmistakable melody from a far distant time as she sang, "Jesus loves me, this I know, for the Bible tells me so. Little ones to Him belong...I belong..."

Then silence. My heart accelerated to a frightening pace,

followed by chills, sweats, trembling, and tears. The disciplined restraint of those past minutes took its measure, exacted its recompense. Now I would surely go to her, interrogate her, get explanations. Former thoughts of not intruding on her reverie were abandoned. I couldn't risk morning. She might be gone. Was she now?

Sadie moved before I could, positioning herself into the curve of Mom's spine.

"It's all right, little girl. Sleep now, Sadie, sleep," she whispered to the watchful dog.

I followed Sadie's lead and settled back in the bed, enchanted by all I had heard. Sleep came in fits and starts, and when Mom stirred with the sun's first light, I hurried the morning ritual, eager for conversation. I opened the blinds, lit the votive candle for devotions, and touched her gnarled hands, which were locked in prayer. Sadie snuggled closer, her big brown eyes gazing adoringly.

"Top o' the morning, Sleepyhead," I greeted my mother as usual.

She smiled that sweet smile, always there, despite the pain, fluttered open her sparkling blue eyes, and sighed, "I'm still here." It was as much a question as a statement, a meek resignation perhaps sprinkled with disappointment.

"Mom, you seemed to be having quite a dream. Do you remember?" It was unfair of me, this feverish rush to question. But my great gnawing fear that the intrusion of the day, the harsh facts of routine, the challenges, the struggle with pain, would cause the magical night to be forgotten, to be gobbled up with necessity's sharp pinch.

"Heaven," she paused and squeezed my hand. Sadie pushed her nose under our fingers as Mom sighed, "Heaven is Christmas."

On this morning, in this moment, that explanation was enough.

Later in the day my brothers and I did talk with her about her dream.

"Paddy, an angel?" Danny, my younger brother, questioned sarcastically.

"Clear hallucination," brother Bart assured.

While I argued the opposite, in favor of Mom's sane, lucid thoughts, she just laughed at the fun her children were having. Bart wondered why she hadn't seen him there—she clearly saw Dad, Danny, and me in the nativity scene. He urged her to go back, look harder in the crowd. Maybe he was tending the camels. She nodded, smiled, and assured him that he would be there. The vision of me in an angelic role and Bart in absentia have provided abundant currency for the family joke bank.

We wanted to press for details, but when her weary eyelids drooped and her weakened body settled deeper beneath the covers, we sensed her desire to keep those treasured dream memories to herself. We respected this, not realizing that these words with her would be among her precious last.

Ten days later, death fulfilled its duty and Mom's suffering ended. As I prepared words of tribute for her funeral service, that wondrous night took clear shape for me, as I understood that she had made a brief trip to heaven and confirmed her belief that heaven *IS* Christmas. Not Santa, and tinsel, and stockings, but the timeless story of that sacred event in Bethlehem. I took for granted all the nativity statues, carvings, and pictures on shelves, in corners, on windowsills, that were ever present in Mom's home, not just at Christmas, but all year. They never came down.

Christmas was not a day or season to her, it was a way of life, a spirit of joy, hope and love, modeled after the Holy Family. She lived the virtues of goodness and grace, guided by her faith, making every day Christmas for all who knew her, with little gifts when least expected—a touch or a kind word. She stayed true to that, even on her last morning.

The votive candle was lit that day, the blinds were opened, and the machine that delivered drugs to soothe her pain clicked, beeped and hummed on.

Mom's eyes remained peacefully closed, one hand held a wooden-bead rosary, the other lay motionless on Sadie's neck. Her face, ever so pale, seemed to have a backlit radiance. Then I noticed the blue-tinged lips. I touched her cheek, and with a trembling shallow final breath, she smiled—an unexpected gift.

In that moment, a powerful scent of roses filled the room for me, but the vase at the statue of Our Lady of Guadalupe held only gardenias.

Forget Me Not
Douglas Wyant

My wife says I've got a selective memory—
I remember only what I want to remember,
not what she expects me to remember.

I'm glad God has a selective memory, too.
He promises to forgive and forget my sins,
but He declares, "I will not forget you!
I have written your name on the palms of my hands."

Sources: 1 John 1:9; Isaiah 43:25; Jeremiah 31:34; Isaiah 49:15, NIV;
Isaiah 49:16, NLT.

A Stolen Mind
Nick West

While taking a walk with my friend, Bill, he plunged into his concerns for his wife's mental lapses. He talked about the time she cooked shrimp and grits for dinner and there were no shrimp.

"Did you forget something?" he asked Karen. The two of them got up and looked in the refrigerator. There was the missing ingredient, right next to the pork chops.

That in and of itself might not have been worth worrying about, but the next week, when three friends arrived to play bridge, Karen was still dressed in her pajamas and housecoat. "Embarrassment," said Bill, "was plain as day on her face."

"It's mostly little things," Bill said. "But she forgets more and more often."

Earlier in the month she had mailed her oldest daughter Jill a birthday present. Not only was the gift sent a week late—a surprise in itself since Karen had always prided herself in keeping up with such things—but the package was returned the next day. She had not remembered the postage.

"Something's going on," Bill said. I could tell he was worried. That afternoon, he called Karen's doctor.

A week passed before I saw Bill again. Over a Waffle House coffee, he shared the news: Karen's MRI had ruled out a brain tumor, but the results of the mental examination stunned him. "She's already passed the early stages of dementia," Bill said. "Soon she's going to need twenty-four hour care. The doctor recommended a facility in Augusta."

Grief suddenly overwhelmed him. He wept silently, but his shoulders trembled.

"I don't know what I will do, and I feel so sorry for Karen. She's the love of my life."

As time went on, Bill divulged that there were more and more times Karen couldn't even recall her daughters' names. She would repeat them over and over, but she couldn't hold on to them for long. He could see he needed to visit Hopewell Manor as soon as possible.

When I telephoned him to see how the trip went, Bill said they'd spent several hours at the facility and had eaten lunch in the dining room. He described the large lobby with Persian rugs, oil paintings, and a huge chandelier. There was a room for Karen across from the nurses' station.

Bill particularly liked Sylvia, one of the administrators. Before Bill and Karen left, she gave him her cell number and told Bill that if he had any questions, he could call her anytime.

On the ride back home, Bill said he tried to engage Karen. "She had nothing to say," he said. "She can't begin to comprehend what's going on."

Bill called Sylvia early the next morning. "I told her to go ahead and send the paperwork," he told me. "I don't really have any other choice."

As promised, Jill and Sissy arrived to help with their mother's move. They packed those things Karen would need, a sad task, and they all drove together to Augusta. Staff members came out to greet them and help Karen get situated in her new quarters. Jill and Sissy strategically placed pictures they'd brought around their mother's room. The ride home must have been heartbreaking for all of them.

Even if he wouldn't admit it, I knew Bill needed a friend. "I'm coming to get you," I said. "Let's walk."

It didn't take many steps for Bill to start talking. "When I hugged Karen goodbye," he said, "I thought maybe I couldn't go through with the whole thing. It was so hard leaving, but thankfully, the girls were with me. I don't think I could have done it without them."

"You and Karen raised them right," I said.

"The staff told me I shouldn't visit her for ten days because it would make it easier for her to adjust. Ten days. That's a long time."

But he did what they asked. He waited exactly ten days.

Bright and early on the eleventh day, Bill came to pick me up. "How was your visit?" I asked.

"To tell you the truth, I'm afraid she's forgotten me. When I walked into the activity room, I was surprised to see Karen sitting closely to another man. Their closeness startled me.

"Finally, she looked up and saw me. She smiled and I went over and gave her a kiss. I persuaded her to go sit with me at a small table, but I couldn't get her to talk with me. If I asked her a question, she'd reply with a yes or a no, but other than that, she said very little. After a few minutes, she just got up and walked away and sat next to her new friend."

"Well," I said, "this has been a big change for you both. Maybe it will be easier the next time."

"I hope so. I'm going back today and check on her."

But the second visit was even more disappointing. Bill hoped Sylvia might have some insight and called to ask if she would see him.

Sylvia was waiting at the front desk when he arrived.

That night, Bill stopped by my house. "I hope you don't mind," he apologized.

"You are always welcome here," I assured him. "Day or night. You know that. Come on, let's sit in the den."

"It was a hard day." He took a seat on the sofa and I sat by him. "I met with Sylvia, the administrator I told you about."

"Sure, I remember. You liked her a lot."

"I do like her, but today she didn't pull any punches. I told her that Karen had attached herself to another resident, and now, she seemed much more interested in spending time with a stranger than me. I wanted to know how this could happen."

"And what did she say to that?"

"She wasn't surprised. She told me Karen is rapidly losing all her memories. She might know me one day and not the next.

Evidently, it's not uncommon for people with Karen's issues to bond with another patient. She told me I had to be realistic. Karen will continue to withdraw, and eventually, she won't know me or the girls." Bill looked away, trying to take control of his emotions.

I knew there was nothing I could say that would make the situation any better. "Sylvia was sympathetic," Bill continued. "She told me she knew how hard it was. 'With dementia,' she said, 'the patient is not the only person who suffers. It affects the whole family.'"

Bill told me he left Sylvia and started down the long hallway to the activity room, not sure what to expect.

"There she was, sitting at the same table with the same guy. I walked over and kissed her on her forehead. She looked right at me, Nick, and I realized no one was at home. Her big eyes were empty. Totally empty. I stayed beside her for an hour, and she never spoke a word to me."

Months went by. Bill went less often to see Karen. "I think I confuse her," he said to me over the phone. "I know it may be pointless for me to visit, but I'm going to visit her whether she knows me or not."

"Why don't I ride with you next time? I mean, if you don't mind some company."

Four days later, we started for Augusta early. Spring was in the air.

"I bet I could find some tulips at a florist," said Bill. "Karen loves tulips."

When we arrived, Bill, carrying a big bouquet of yellow and purple flowers in his arms, went up to see Karen. I waited in the lobby, fearing that my presence would disorient her even more. I thumbed mindlessly through a magazine, feeling blessed that my own wife still knew and loved me. Hardly any time passed before I looked up to see the elevator doors opening. The tulips dropped from Bill's hands as he stepped from the elevator.

"I tried to kiss her," he said, "but she has no idea who I am."

We heard the elevator, opening and closing, opening and closing. The doors were tearing the tulips apart.

.

All sorrows can be borne if you put them into a
story or tell a story about them.
Isak Dinesen

A Gift

Jayne Padgett Bowers

When the seeds were germinating for this anthology, I found myself concerned about our common theme. Was it the passing of seasons? The age-old story of the law of the harvest? Or was it simply life's changes and the people who accompany us along the road? Then one afternoon as I was mulling over the issue while working at Habitat ReStore, Maureen Renaud, a fellow volunteer showed me a beautiful photograph of a barn and told me a little bit about the man who captured the image of the time-worn structure with the birds swooping around it. I was entranced.

"There must be story here," I told Maureen.

"There is. Would you like to read it sometime?"

"Yes…and soon. Like this week," I told her.

As soon as I began reading "The Barn," I was touched by its power and significance. I could see that while this was Art Shealy's story, it was a universal one that would resonate with everyone. Indeed the story was a gift that tied our work together. My feelings about the barn echo these words of Art's:

Look around you. There are countless abandoned buildings, tobacco barns, homes large and small. Have you ever wondered what stories they could tell—if only they could talk? One day they're in place, just as we have seen them for decades, albeit a bit worse for the weather. The next day they're gone, victims of a microburst storm or some other modern calamity, or maybe they've just collapsed under their own weight. As I think about these things, I'm reminded how much we are all like the old structures. One day here and vital, the next day gone.

The Barn
Art Shealy

I remember it like it was yesterday—my birth.

There was the smell of freshly sawn wood, and the sweat of ten neighbors who pitched in to help. The smell of disturbed earth. The unmistakable smell of congratulatory Lucky Strikes and, if I'm not mistaken, the faint smell of corn liquor.

The last nail was driven with an exuberance that said clearly, "This barn's not going anywhere."

And here I've stood—for how long now?

I don't know how I came to be, I just am. But once here, I was proud to be and do whatever my master wanted.

Countless nights I have been a base of operations for Mama and Papa Owl and a shelter for their off-spring. Once in a while, a king snake would come along and offer to rid my premises of mice in exchange for shade from the Carolina sun. And it being nature's way, four-legged visitors of the feline persuasion came looking for a meal. On more than a few occasions, they left off a litter of kittens for me to watch over.

Then there were the human visitors—not the ones who had their tools and next year's seed corn stored safely under my roof, but the smaller ones who used to find places to hide inside my walls while others looked for them. I was the fort from which they defended the homestead against marauding Northern Blue Coats. I was King Arthur's castle.

But they soon grew up. Life became more serious for them. Within the confines of my walls, they tried their first cigarettes. Beneath my roof there were lovers' trysts. And for those who ventured too far from the straight and narrow, there was a mystical area somewhere to my rear, where work-weary dads would explain the finer points of Southern manners.

Throughout my useful life, I stood stalwart against the bite of the winter winds, the swelter of mid-August afternoons, always providing shelter and safety. After all, I was constructed of the finest materials. My job was to endure—to be timeless in an ever-changing world.

My demise began almost imperceptibly. A loose piece of roofing tin creaked and moaned in the March wind. A hinge that held in place a protective door, rusted, now broken due to oxidation for the lack of a drop of oil.

The hand-hewn joints and wooden pegs held the four corners of my log frame together; solid heart pine covered my exterior. I was the pride of the men who built me. Now my timber frame and my wooden skin are cracked and sagging. From the looks of me, my days appear numbered.

But wait! Can it be that I'm still of some use in this world? A migrating flock of black birds thinks so. They stop in for a meal and some rest, safe within my protective walls.

Just when I thought I was done for, I feel a spark of life. I still have something to contribute.

Winter Showdown
Lyrics, Paddy Bell

Bleary-eyed morn
daughter of the dawn,
rubs away the sandman's telltale crusted signs.

Her spring hounds chase
every wintry trace,
signal that the jasmine seek the sky-lit pines.

Brittle branches soften, tender vines unwind,
skitter up to heights they've never known.
Blossoms open shyly, blinking at the light,
leapfrog in a race to reach the sun.

Bitter gust of roguish wind says it's not done.
Morning larks twitter,
showdown with winter has begun.

Slicing the air,
trumpet flowers blare,
drown out wintry weary drearisome refrain.

Promises and purpose cannot be denied.
Laws of nature have no in-between.
Former fears forgotten, hesitation lost,
jasmine ever faithful, evergreen.

Sudden banks of charcoal clouds eclipse the sun.
Morning larks twitter,
showdown with winter has begun.

Is There a Cook in the House?

"Anybody can cook," my wife says. "All you have to do is follow the instructions. But your *want-to* has to work."

When someone says, "I can't," Gail asks, "Are your hands put on backwards?"

Douglas Wyant

Recipes

If we don't sing the songs, tell the stories, and make the foods that are dear to us, our children won't know what they missed, but I think they'll miss it just the same.

Laura Ward Branca

Low Country Boil for a Crowd

My son Mark made this for my birthday celebration last spring. Here is his recipe.

Myra Yeatts

20 pounds of deveined shrimp. Leave tails on. Shrimp loses flavor when cooked without tails.
10-pound bag of small red potatoes (though you may want to use only 8 pounds), cut in quarters
6 onions
6 heads of garlic
12 lemons, halved
2 bunches of rough-cut celery (do not discard leaves; use in cooking)
24 ears of corn on the cob broken in half
5 packages of kielbasa-cut into 1-inch pieces
One tablespoon Zatarain's Liquid Shrimp Crab Boil concentrate for each five pounds of shrimp (or to taste)

Fill a very large pot (20-gallons or more) half full of water. Add Zatarain concentrate. Bring water to boil and add potatoes and celery. Cook for fifteen minutes, then add sausage. Cook for an additional five minutes before adding corn. Cook three minutes.

Add shrimp and cook only three to four minutes more, just until shrimp turns pink.

Serves 50

Ollie's Favorite Chow-Chow

Fermenting and canning are all the rage again. Apparently pickles of all sorts are good for you and your digestion. This recipe is from Ollie Croxton's collection. Formerly of Kershaw, Mrs. Croxton, who taught school for many years, now lives in Laurens with her daughter Jane.

12 large onions
12 bell peppers
12 red, hot peppers (or less, for a milder relish)
½ gallon chopped green tomatoes
4 tablespoons ground mustard
1 tablespoon turmeric
1 tablespoon ground ginger
4 tablespoons mustard seed
3 tablespoons celery seed
2 tablespoons whole mixed pickling spices
2 to 3 quarts of vinegar

Chop or grate cabbage, onions and peppers. Chop green tomatoes. Mix vegetables with salt and allow to stand overnight. The next day, drain thoroughly.

Tie whole spices into a small piece of cheesecloth. Place the spice bag, ground spices, sugar and vinegar in a large pot. Simmer for twenty minutes before adding drained vegetables. Continue to simmer until very hot throughout and well-seasoned, about ten to fifteen minutes. Remove spice bag.

Ladle hot mixture into sterile jars, leaving 1/8 inch headspace. Adjust lids by wiping the rims clean, putting the lid on with gasket side down next to glass. Screw metal bands firmly over lids and tighten.

Submerge jars in simmering water for ten minutes.

Serve with dried peas and beans, pulled pork, hot dogs or ham.

Strange to see how a good dinner
and feasting reconciles everybody.
Samuel Pepys

Hidden Ingredient Cake

Cereal, sauerkraut, Coca-Cola, Ritz crackers have all found their way as secret ingredients into cookies, cakes, and pies in my family. As for this cake recipe, we say, "Why eat chocolate when you can have zucchini?"

Paddy Bell

4 ounces unsweetened chocolate
4 large eggs
3 cups sugar
1 ½ cups salad oil
3 cups all-purpose flour
1 teaspoon baking powder
1 teaspoon salt
1 teaspoon baking soda
3 cups grated zucchini
1 cup chopped pecans

Melt the chocolate over low heat in a medium sauce pan. Stir frequently to avoid burning. Set aside to cool.

Beat eggs until thick and light colored; add the sugar, oil, and cooled chocolate. Mix to combine.

In another bowl, combine flour, baking soda, salt, baking powder and mix well. Add to the wet ingredients, mixing well.

Stir in the zucchini and pecans.

Pour into greased and floured Bundt pan and bake at 350 degrees for one hour and fifteen minutes, or until knife inserted in the cake comes out clean.

Cool for ten minutes on wire rack; then turn cake out onto rack to cool completely. Sprinkle top with confectioner's sugar.

Thelma's Big Black Walnut Pound Cake
> *Ex-mother-in-laws—lots of us have them. Mine was named Thelma. She was a fabulous cook.*
>
> *Kathryn Etters Lovatt*

3 cups all-purpose flour
2 cups brown sugar
1 teaspoon baking powder
3 sticks butter
5 eggs
1 cup milk
1 teaspoon vinegar
1 teaspoon vanilla extract
6 to 8 ounces finely ground black walnuts

Preheat oven to 325 degrees.

Mix all ingredients above, alternating dry and liquid ingredients. Prepare one ten-inch tube pan by greasing and flouring (or, the updated way, using baking spray).

Bake for one hour and a half or until a toothpick comes out clean. The top should be brown and crusty. Cool on a rack for ten minutes before removing from pan.

If you can wait a day (nearly impossible), cut this cake after the black walnuts have had an opportunity to release their oils and spread their flavor throughout. Serves a dozen or more.

Mexican Scramble

Mom would start making batches of this popular snack on her birthday, December 12, to give as gifts throughout the Christmas season. She would package in festive tins and jars, tie on a bow and a sprig of holly, and have them ready for friends, neighbors, family, the postman, the milkman, the egg lady, and the newspaper boy.

Paddy Bell

1 box (8 ounces) very thin pretzels
2 cups salad oil
2 pounds mixed salted nuts
2 tablespoons Worcestershire sauce
1 package (3 cups) Wheat Chex cereal
1 teaspoon garlic salt
I package (3 cups) Cheerios cereal
1 tablespoon seasoned salt
1 package (3 cups) Rice Chex cereal

Mix all ingredients in very large roaster, bake in very slow oven (250 degrees) for two hours, stirring and turning mixture with **wooden** spoon every fifteen minutes (be careful not to crush cereals). Makes about 8 quarts. Cool and store in airtight containers.

Lemon Chess Pie
This recipe from the industrious and gentle Shakers of Pleasant Hill, Kentucky, is over 100 years old.

Paddy Bell

4 eggs
1 tablespoon white cornmeal
1 ½ cups sugar
1 tablespoon flour
1 tablespoon grated lemon rind
¼ cup milk
¼ cup lemon juice
¼ cup melted butter
Pinch of salt

Beat eggs; gradually add sugar. Stir in remaining ingredients. Pour into an unbaked nine-inch pie shell.

Bake at 350 degrees for forty minutes or until brown.

Do not overbake.

Elephant Stew
Just for fun.
Paddy Bell

1 elephant
2 rabbits (optional)
Salt and pepper to taste

Cut elephant into small bite-size pieces. This should take about two months.

Add enough brown gravy to cover.

Cook over kerosene fire at 465 degrees for four weeks.

This will serve 3,800 people. If more are expected, two rabbits may be added.

Wild Duck
For lovers of game.
Nick West

4 wild duck breasts, skin and fat removed
½ cup orange marmalade
½ or more cups red wine (enough to cover)
Bacon

Place duck breasts in a shallow pan. Mix wine and marmalade and pour over the duck. Cover with plastic wrap and place in refrigerator for two hours.

Wrap two pieces of bacon around each breast pinning it with tooth picks.

Grill on an open grill for twelve to fifteen minutes on each side.

Cranberry Chutney
My mother Louise Bevan has been making this for Thanksgiving and Christmas ever since I was a child. She has no idea where she got the recipe, but once you've had it you'll never again be satisfied with anything out of a can.

I usually double the batch at Thanksgiving and it keeps well in the refrigerator through Christmas. It's a popular side-dish to turkey and is often added to sandwiches. It goes fast.
Brenda Bevan Remmes

Put into a large pot on top of the stove:

3-4 small oranges peeled and cut into pieces
4 cups of raw cranberries
2 cups of sugar
1 chopped unpeeled apple
½ cup seedless raisins
½ cup orange juice
¼ cup of chopped nuts
1 tablespoon vinegar
½ teaspoon of ginger
½ teaspoon cinnamon

Heat to boiling and then simmer uncovered until cranberries pop and are cooked.

Continue to simmer to desired thickness.

Refrigerate.

Makes five cups.

Fruitcake Cookies
> *Children of all ages, who turn their noses up at fruitcake, scarf up these fruitcake cookies. My wife makes a batch of them for Christmas every year.*
>
> *This recipe has been handed down in her family from sister to sister and mother to daughter for years. No one is sure where it originated. Gail's stained, handwritten copy is dated 12-14-80.*
>
> *Douglas Wyant*

1 pound chopped walnuts
1 pound candied pineapple
1 pound candied cherries
1 pound pitted dates
3/4 pound golden raisins
1 cup butter
3 eggs, well-beaten
1 cup light brown sugar
3 cups plain flour
1 teaspoon baking soda
1 teaspoon cinnamon
½ cup milk
2 tablespoons sherry extract
1 cup cooking sherry

Chop fruit. Soak overnight in the cup of cooking sherry.

Cream butter and sugar.

Add beaten eggs.

Sift in flour, baking soda, and cinnamon.

Add milk and sherry extract.

Fold in nuts and fruits.

Put heaping spoonfuls of cookie mixture on a baking stone or well-greased cookie sheet and bake at 300 degrees for twenty to twenty-five minutes.

Makes approximately twelve dozen cookies.

And when you crush an apple with your teeth, say to it in your heart:
Your seeds shall live in my body,
And the buds of your tomorrow shall blossom in my heart,
And your fragrance shall be my breath,
And together we shall rejoice through all the seasons.
Kahlil Gibran

Turnip, Leek and Cauliflower Soup
This is a comforting, healthy winter soup.
S. Jane Gari

1-quart vegetable stock
3-4 medium sized leeks, cleaned with dark green sections removed
Sea salt and pepper to taste
3 large turnips, with purple skins peeled
1 head of cauliflower
3 cups unsweetened almond milk (You may substitute soy or hemp, but almond tastes best in this recipe.)
½ tsp thyme
1 tablespoon snipped/chopped chives

Chop the washed leeks into small pieces. In a six-quart saucepan over medium heat, add one and a half cups of the vegetable broth. Add the leeks and a heavy pinch of salt and sweat on medium-high heat for five minutes. Decrease the heat to medium-low and cook until the leeks are tender, approximately twenty-five minutes, stirring occasionally.

Add the turnips, cauliflower and the rest of the vegetable broth; then increase the heat to medium-high, and bring to a boil. Reduce the heat to low, cover, and gently simmer until the turnips and cauliflower are soft, approximately thirty-five minutes.

Remove from heat and puree the mixture in a blender until smooth. Stir in the almond milk. Taste and adjust seasoning if desired. Sprinkle with chives and serve.

Makes about one and a half quarts of soup.

001A:

Speckled Butter Beans

Some people cook these beans with a ham hock, but in my family, only dried lima beans were cooked with ham. A very good substitute for the fat meat is uncured bacon. Any fresh or fresh-frozen beans may be prepared this way.

On the off-chance that you have beans left over, make succotash: Sauté a half to one cup of following: sliced okra, corn, chopped sweet onion and red pepper (plus a slice of cooked and chopped bacon if you like). Add beans. Season with salt, pepper and a teaspoon of butter.

Kathryn Etters Lovatt

Bring 2 cups of water to boil with a two-inch piece of thick fatback or streak-of-lean.
Add a good shake of salt and a couple of grinds of pepper.

After the liquid comes to a full rolling boil, cover and reduce heat.

Simmer for thirty minutes. (This, in fancy terms, is sometimes called an enhanced broth. Do not skip this step—it will make the difference between bland and flavorful.)

Add one pound of fresh or fresh-frozen speckled butter beans.

Cook on medium-low about forty-five minutes to an hour, adding more water if necessary.

The beans are ready when they are soft with a buttery texture.

Miss Marvell's Cheese-Garlic Biscuits
These are the biscuits I loved when I attended Thomas Sumter Academy. Enjoy and be blessed!
John Aldrich

2 cups Original Bisquick mix
2/3 cup milk
½ cup shredded Cheddar cheese (2 ounces)
2 tablespoons butter or margarine
1/8 teaspoon garlic powder

Heat oven to 450 degrees.
Stir Bisquick mix, milk, and cheese until soft dough forms.
Drop dough by nine spoonfuls onto ungreased cookie sheet.
Bake eight to ten minutes until golden brown.
Stir together butter and garlic powder, brush over warm biscuits.

Australian Pavlova

This beautiful dessert was created in honor of the Russian ballerina Anna Pavlova during her 1920's tour of Australia and New Zealand. Katherine McCaughan, who shared this recipe, grew up in Australia. Her book, Natasha Lands Down Under, *took a first place in the Moonbeam Children's Book Awards in the young adult/historical/cultural section.*

Meringue Base

4 egg whites
1 cup sugar
1 level teaspoon vinegar
½ teaspoon vanilla

Heat oven to 225 degrees. Grease flat cookie sheet.

Beat egg whites until stiff, add sugar till silky, then quickly beat in vinegar and vanilla.

Place mixture on cookie sheet in a circular pile.

Bake in heated oven just below center for one hour and thirty minutes. Turn oven off.

Leave meringue in oven for one hour and thirty minutes, with the door oven opened slightly, or leave in the oven overnight with door closed. It should cool slowly.

Just before serving, fill center of meringue with sweetened whipped cream, strawberries and passion fruit or other preferred fruit.

Elvis Presley's Famous Peanut Butter Sandwich

On a recent trip to Graceland, I learned that Elvis' peanut butter sandwich was a classic held in high esteem by millions. Upon my return to South Carolina, my finding was verified by dozens of his fans living in our community. I hope this recipe borrowed from a postcard in a Graceland gift shop will delight the palates of "The King's" admirers.

Jayne Padgett Bowers

2 large bananas
6 slices white bread
½ cup butter (one stick)
1 cup peanut butter

Peel and mash bananas.

Mix peanut butter with bananas thoroughly. Toast bread slightly and spread mix on bread. Melt butter in skillet and brown sandwiches on each side slowly until golden brown.

A Few of Emma's Christmas Cookie Recipes

My mother-in-law Emma Remmes, subject of my stories in this anthology, raised her family on home-cooked meals and plenty of ice cream and desserts. At the beginning of the Christmas season, rarely a day went by that she didn't have a new variety of cookies in the oven. These would be added to the Christmas day platter. It was considered a family tradition.

Woe to me, the daughter-in-law who failed to understand the importance of this ritual. In an effort to politely ignore my shortcomings, Emma mailed a box of homemade cookies to our house every year. After her death, my husband's Aunt Vera Mae immediately picked up the tradition. They both liked me for other reasons, thank goodness, and considered my failure to celebrate the holidays without the customary kitchen edibles something they'd overlook.

They did, however, leave recipes lying around "just in case" I might want to try one or two. To be honest, I have, but most don't taste like the ones Bill's mother made. I think it has to do with "lard," but as Kathryn once wrote, very possibly "the bit of love that was added to the bowl."

So here are some of the recipes. I hope they all taste as wonderful as I remember.

Brenda Bevan Remme

Emma's Fudge

1 box powdered sugar
½ cup cocoa
¼ teaspoon salt
4 tablespoons milk
6 tablespoons butter
1 tablespoon vanilla
1 cup chopped nuts (pecans or walnuts)

Sift together the powdered sugar and cocoa and salt. Combine all the ingredients (except nuts) in a double boiler.

Place over simmering water and stir until smooth. Add nuts and mix. Spread quickly in buttered eight-by-eight pan or an eight-by-eight buttered Christmas tin.

Let sit until it hardens. No need to put in refrigerator, but cover well.

Emma's Divinity

There are lots of theories about how to make good divinity. Emma never made it on rainy days or when the humidity was too high. I've heard others say that's "silly." You should be able to make good divinity any time. Honestly, the few times I've tried, I've only gotten it to taste as good as Emma's once.

2 ½ cups sugar
½ cup water
½ cup white syrup
2 egg whites
1 teaspoon vanilla

Cook syrup, water and sugar to soft ball stage when tested in cold water.

Beat egg whites and vanilla until stiff, but not dry.

Pour half of cooked syrup mixture a bit at a time over egg whites while beating them.

Return other half of syrup to stove top and boil to hard crack stage.

Slowly pour hard crack stage syrup mixture into original mixture while still beating. Beat until shiny and it holds its shape. If it gets too thick, add drops of hot water.

Pour into a buttered dish or drop in spoonfuls onto wax paper.

Place a pecan on top of each piece.

(Some people pour chopped nuts into mixture instead of placing pecan on top.)

Emma's Very Favorite Sugar Cookies
These are my family's favorite cookies. They disappear quickly.

1 cup butter
2 eggs
1 cup of sugar
½ teaspoon vanilla
3 cups of all-purpose flour
½ teaspoon baking soda
½ teaspoon baking powder
Sprinkles if desired

Sift together flour, soda, baking powder.

Using a pastry blender, sometimes called a pastry cutter, "cut" butter into flour mixture. Don't "mix" these ingredients, but "cut" them in so that the flour mixture looks like little pebbles when you're done. I've used two knives on occasion and simply crisscrossed them until I get the desired size.

Add eggs to flour-butter mixture and mix with electric mixer.

Chill.

Roll out as thin as you like (the thinner the tastier), and cut into shapes with cookie cutters. I often just use a biscuit cutter but sometimes do Christmas trees and Santas.

At Christmas time, I sprinkle with colored sugar sprinkles.

Bake 375 for eight to ten minutes on ungreased cookie sheets. (Careful—if very thin, cookies may cook faster.)

Emma's Snickerdoodles
Another family favorite.

1 cup soft shortening
2 eggs
1 ½ cups sugar
2 ¾ cups sifted flour
2 teaspoons cream of tartar
1 teaspoon baking soda
½ teaspoon salt

Coating:

2 tablespoons granulated sugar
2 teaspoons cinnamon

Mix shortening, eggs and sugar.

Sift together flour, cream of tartar, soda and salt and stir into shortening mixture.

Chill dough.

Roll into balls about the size of walnuts and roll them in a mixture of granulated sugar and cinnamon.

Place about two-inches apart on ungreased cookie sheet.

Bake at 400 degrees for eight to ten minutes until lightly browned but still soft. They will puff up at first and then flatten.

Emma's Hello Dollies
This recipe has been around for many years. I doubt that it is original but it was one of her annual selections.

Melt in a baking pan:
¼ cup margarine

Pat 1 cup graham cracker crumbs over melted margarine

Sprinkle in layers over the top:
1 cup flaked coconut
1 cup chocolate chips
1 cup butterscotch chips
1 cup chopped nuts
1 can sweetened condensed milk (drizzled over the top of everything)

Bake at 325 degrees for thirty to forty minutes.

Emma's Gingersnaps
Perfect for the holidays.

¾ cup soft shortening
1 cup brown sugar
1 egg
¼ cup molasses
2 cups flour
¼ teaspoon salt
2 teaspoons soda
1 teaspoon each of ginger, cinnamon, cloves
granulated sugar

Combine shortening, sugar and egg in bowl.

Beat well.

Add molasses and beat again.

Sift dry ingredients together and add to mixture. Mix well.

Chill dough well. Shape into one-inch balls and roll in granulated sugar.

Place two-inches apart on greased baking sheet.

Bake at 350 degrees for twelve to fifteen minutes.

Heavenly Brownies with Frosting and a Marshmallow Twist
One more of Emma's favorites.

1 ½ stick butter
2 eggs
¾ cup plain flour
1 cup sugar
3 tablespoons cocoa
1 cup chopped nuts
Miniature marshmallows

Cream butter and sugar, and one at a time, beating after each one.

Add flour and cocoa. Mix well. Add chopped nuts.

Pour into nine-by-thirteen-inch pan and bake at 350 degrees for twenty to twenty-five minutes.

Remove from oven and pour miniature marshmallows over brownies. Return to oven on broil and stick them in one to two minutes until toasted.

Ice the brownies after they have cooled with the mixture below:

2 cups sugar
1 stick butter
½ cup cocoa
½ cup evaporated milk
1 teaspoon vanilla
1 teaspoon butter

Melt butter and add the other ingredients. Mix thoroughly.
Bring to rolling boil and boil for one minute.
Remove from heat and add one teaspoon vanilla and the extra
teaspoon butter.
Beat until it's a consistency to pour over brownies.

Cool and slice.

Docia's Birthday Pie

My mom saved all of my grandmother's recipes, although many of them were written on scraps of paper or on the backs of envelopes. Now I have inherited those tattered keepsakes along with my own mother's collection. Most of them are full of assumptions, providing only a list of ingredients and not a word of instruction. I could fill a book with recipe titles followed by vague ideas, but what I offer instead is this pie. My mother's roommate in nursing school, Docia Mcleod, once told my Mama in advance of her birthday, "All I want is one of your chocolate pies."

Kathryn Etters Lovatt

For the pie:

2 squares (2 ounces) unsweetened chocolate
1 cup light brown sugar
3 tablespoons all-purpose flour
3 eggs, separated, saving whites
1 ½ cups milk, scalded
2 tablespoons butter
1 teaspoon vanilla
1 baked pastry shell

Melt chocolate in double boiler.

Mix sugar, flour, egg yolks and milk. Add to melted chocolate and continue to cook over double boiler, stirring constantly, until thickened.

Remove from heat and add butter. Cool while preparing meringue.

Meringue:

Reserved egg whites
6 tablespoons granulated sugar

Beat egg whites until stiff, adding two tablespoons of the sugar at a time.

Pour chocolate filling into baked crust and cover with meringue. Bake about fifteen minutes or until golden brown in a 325 degree oven.

Makes one nine-inch pie.

Cassoulet Italiene

Serve this dish with grated parmesan, Romano and/or asiago cheeses. This recipe also works well in the crock pot and tastes especially good served with sourdough rolls or a crusty rustico.

Laura Bruno Lilly

4 hot Italian sausage links (I use 2 each of Canino's & Boulder Sausage Brands, but for my Southern Cooks, use Johnsonville brand hot Italian sausage)

2-3 chicken breasts with skin & bones -OR- 3-4 chicken thighs with skin & bones

1 large onion, thinly sliced

2 green bell peppers, thinly sliced

3 garlic cloves, each quartered

1 can ceci beans (also known as chickpeas)

1 large can whole peeled Italian tomatoes

1teaspoon chicken Better Than Bouillon, or 1 cube chicken bouillon

½-1 can water (using tomato can to measure)

2-3 potatoes, thinly sliced

½ pound mushrooms, each halved

Olive oil, basil, paprika, black pepper, garlic salt

Brown sausages. Cut in bite-sized pieces and place in large casserole dish. (I use my large oval French Corning ware.)

Add olive oil as needed to skillet to sauté onion, green peppers, and garlic cloves, and add to casserole.

Add more olive oil as needed to the skillet to sear both sides of the chicken. Add to casserole (they will not be thoroughly cooked at this point).

Sprinkle crushed basil over remaining liquids in hot pan and allow to season on medium heat.

Carefully add the can of tomatoes and, while the flavors blend, cut the tomatoes in the pan. Pour all into the casserole.

Add the extra water and the chicken bouillon to the hot pan and swirl to get all the juices and allow the bouillon to fully incorporate. Pour the mixture over the casserole and add remaining spices to taste.

Add the sliced potatoes and mix all together, leaving the chicken, skin side down, on top of everything. Cover casserole and cook in 350 degrees oven for one and a half to two hours.

Remove from oven and take out the chicken to cool before peeling off the meat. Add the mushrooms and the deboned chicken meat to the casserole and cook for another half hour or more until totally cooked through.

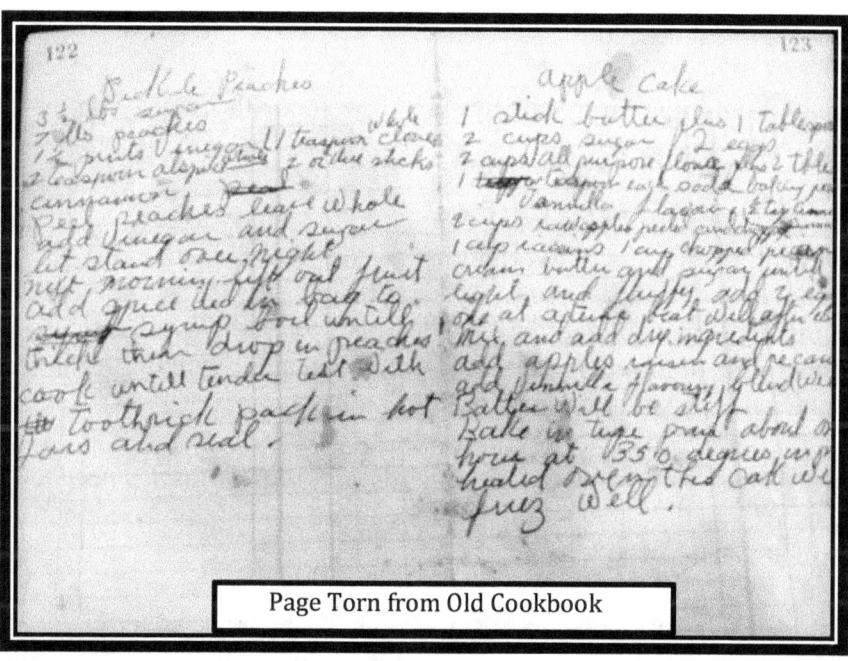

Page Torn from Old Cookbook

My Original Mother for Sour Dough Bread

Laura Bruno Lilly

Basic instructions on how to begin a sourdough starter from scratch:

1 packet dry yeast (or 1 heaping tablespoon loose yeast)
2 cups warm water
2 cups unbleached flour

Empty yeast into non-metallic mixing bowl and stir in water until dissolved.

Add flour until well blended. Cover with lid slightly askew, let stand at room temperature for forty-eight hours. Mother will become bubbly and develop a slightly yellowish liquid on top; this is just the beginning. It may take a few days or weeks to establish a foamy, tangy Mother. Use your nose and eyes to guide you along with the addition of one half cup water & one cup flour on day three.

Feel free to 'stir down' the bubbling mass as it incorporates needed bacteria from the surrounding air. Of course, placing the bowl in a warm area helps, too.

After day four, use one cup of starter to bake a 'first' batch of sourdough bread of any sort, replenishing with one cup flour, one cup milk, one-third cup sugar and beginning the cycle of feeding every four to five days.

"Easy" Sourdough Bread

This bread inspired a poem. We once had neighbors that were Ecuadoran and only one person spoke English. They were fantastic neighbors and we communicated regularly throughout our daily lives. My poem follows this recipe.

Laura Bruno Lilly

Use my original recipe for mother or any other starter to make this bread.

1 packet (1 tablespoon) dry yeast
¼ cup warm water
1 teaspoon sugar
1 egg
¼ cup vegetable oil
½ cup water
1 teaspoon salt
1/3 cup sugar
1 cup Mother*
3 ½ cups all-purpose flour

Dissolve yeast in warm water, stirring in the one teaspoon of sugar. Allow to sit for fifteen minutes.

Mix the egg, vegetable oil, water, salt and one-third cup sugar in a large mixing bowl. Add Mother to the egg mixture along with the yeast mixture. With electric mixer thoroughly blend in two cups of the flour. Add remaining flour and mix with a wooden spoon.

Turn onto floured board and knead ten to twenty times. Add a bit more flour if still sticky. Put dough in greased mixing bowl, turning it to make sure the top of the dough is greased in the process. Cover bowl with cloth and let rise two hours in a warm place.

After dough has risen to double in bulk punch down and pour onto floured board and knead again for two minutes. Divide into two balls to shape into bread or rolls and place on well-greased baking sheets. Cover and let rise two more hours in a warm place.

Just before placing in oven, slit tops of loaves. Bake at 350-degrees for about twenty to twenty-five minutes, but keep an eye out because each oven is different—it may take longer.

*Feed Mother every four to five days and each time after starter has been used in a recipe with: one cup flour, one cup milk, one-third cup sugar. Set on counter or in fridge with top slightly askew. Starter can be frozen (but doesn't always thaw-out back alive!) just be sure to thaw one or two days before use and to replenish before freezing.

Also, Mother does not like anything metallic!

It was only a loaf of bread
Laura Bruno Lilly

One loaf
out of four
(baked to imperfection).
One loaf
chosen
(the one most round; least browned).
Bridging our door
to theirs
(some 30 steps away).
Three of five
arrive next morning
(their door to ours).
Hand-delivering
note of thanks
(smiling faces all around).
One loaf
out of four
(baked warmth shared).

Camden Writers

L to R: John Aldrich, Paddy Bell, Mindy Blakely, Jayne Padgett Bowers, Ashley Carmichael

L to R: Vanessa Friedrich, S. Jane Gari, LaShella Kirkland, Martha Dabbs Greenway, Laura Bruno Lilly

L to R: Kathryn Etters Lovatt,
Brenda Bevan Remmes
Nick West,
Douglas Wyant,
Myra Yeatts

John W. Aldrich is a graduate of the University of South Carolina with a B.A. in the Liberal Arts. His first college essay won *The Final Draft* contest at Francis Marion University. His short fiction appears in *Storyteller Magazine* April/May/June 2015 Issue and *Morpheus Tales,* February 2016, Issue # 28.

Paddy Bell's first writing endeavor, *DOGS: The Musical*, culminated in a run at the renowned Piccolo Spoleto Arts Festival. This success, due in great part to her collaboration with Dick Goodwin as composer/arranger, launched a writing interest that spans the genres of screenplay, short story, children's literature, and musical text.

The Goodwin/Bell team recently received rave reviews for their jazz creation, *Jasmine Rhythms*, and in March, 2017, their commissioned symphony, *Timeless Banks*, will premiere at Southeast Missouri State University.

Paddy holds a BA degree in Interdisciplinary Studies and is an alumnus of the Creative Theatre Institute, New York. Her publications have appeared in *The Petigru Review, Serving Up Memory* and in guest columns for *The Chronicle-Independent.*

Mindy Blakely, an avid reader of mysteries and romance stories, holds a Bachelor of Science degree in business Administration from Winthrop University in Rock Hill, SC. The International Library of Poetry published two of her poems, "Alone Again," and "First Kiss" in their anthologies titled *Outstanding Poets of 1998* and *Traces of Yesterday.*

Jayne Padgett Bowers is a semi-retired educator who teaches online courses and writes a little each day. First place winner in the 2016 Carrie McCray Nonfiction Award, Jayne's work has appeared in the *Ensign, Guideposts*, and *The Petigru Review*. She's the author of a textbook, *Human Relations in Industry* (1989), and has published *Musings of a Missionary Mom, Eve's Sisters*, and *Crossing the Bridge: Succeeding in a Community College and Beyond. Follow her @jaynepbowers and* www.jaynebowers.com.

Ashley M. Carmichael earned a Bachelor of Arts in English from the University of North Carolina Wilmington, graduating Summa Cumme Laude. As a North Carolina Teaching Fellow Alumna and veteran teacher, Ashley remains devoted to life-long learning and has participated in two National Endowment for the Humanities travel grants, taken financial literacy and art classes, and enjoys traveling worldwide all as a way to embrace new experiences and grow as a writer. Her first novel, *Valerie's Vow,* debuted in 2014. Ashley currently lives near Columbia, SC with her dog, a beautiful pit-bull named Emma. Follow Ashley on her blog (www.ashleymcarmichael.com), Facebook and Twitter (@amcarmichael13), or email ashleymcarmichaelauthor@gmail.com

Vanessa Friedrich is a professional equestrian and native German who has lived in the United States since 2002. After recovering from a severe horse riding accident, she wrote her first book, *Determination or Just Plain Stubbornness.* An excerpt from this book was published in a recent volume of *Chicken Soup for the Soul* and in this anthology. Vanessa is a therapeutic riding instructor and equine specialist.

S. Jane Gari lives in Elgin, South Carolina with her husband and daughter. Three adapted chapters from her memoir, *Losing the Dollhouse* were nominated for the Pushcart Prize. The first chapter of her forthcoming novel, *Shakespeare's Daughters*, has also been nominated for a Pushcart. Her *Idiot's Guide to the Healthy Gut* launched in May 2016 with Alpha Books (a division of Penguin/Random House). Jane has also co-written *Flush This* Book, a collection of humorous essays.

Martha Dabbs Greenway is a seventh generation South Carolinian and resides at Dabbs Crossroads in a rambling country house built by her granddaddy. Martha's reflections on life also appear in the anthologies produced by Southern Sampler Artists Colony, *A Southern Sampler* and *Charleston and the South.* Co-founder of the Southern Sampler Artists Colony and retired Director of the Sumter County Cultural Commission, Martha lives contentedly with her cats, Sonoma and Salem.

LaShella Kirkland was born in Camden, SC and graduated from North Central High School. She attended East Carolina University in Greenville, NC where she studied music; however, after two years, and failing music theory, she decided to major in Communications with a minor in Theater and Speech. Following graduation, she headed to Wilmington, NC, aka "Wilmywood," to pursue a career in acting. Kirkland worked as a movie extra in "T-Bone and Weasel", "Super Mario Brothers", and "Matlock." In 1994, she decided to study for a second degree in history at the University of North Carolina at Wilmington. She focused on both Native American and African American Studies and Cultures. Her genre of writing is non-fiction, but she loves the 'peculiars' of her own racial and southern background. What has she learned? Our similarities are just as hilarious as our differences.

Laura Bruno Lilly Alongside her music, writing has been a faithful companion giving Laura a great excuse to exploit the virtues of caffeine. Her articles and reviews have appeared in publications such as *The Rosette, The Mandolin Journal,* and the *GFA Soundboard. She* received the 2016 Liebster Blogging Award. Laura is currently working on completing a book of creative non-fiction and has been awarded a Puffin Grant to record its accompanying music. Originally from Colorado, she is now resides in Florence, SC. www.laurabrunolilly.com

Kathryn Etters Lovatt earned her MA in English and creative writing from Hollins University. She continued studies at Hong Kong University where she taught American Studies. A former winner of North Carolina's Doris Betts Prize, she also won Press 53's short fiction competition and three Carrie McCray Awards from SCWA. A Virginia Center for the Arts fellow, she is a former recipient of the SC Art Commission's Individual Artist grant for prose. Most recently, her work has appeared in *NC Literary Review* on-line, *Serving Up Memory,* and *His Mother (*Southern Sass Publishing Alliances), which first published "The Pioneering Spirit". Lovatt resides in Camden, SC. (kathrynlovatt@hotmail.com).

Brenda Bevan Remmes lives near the Black River Swamp in South Carolina in an old family home filled with the history of generations past. Her debut novel, *The Quaker Café*, has sold over 120,000 copies worldwide. Her second novel, *Home to Cedar Branch,* was published by Lake Union Publishing in 2016. Brenda has also written two family memoirs: *Everything Happens at the Crossroad*s and *Emma.* brendaremmes@gmail.com

Nick West, a former resident of Wisacky, South Carolina, has recently relocated to Anderson to be near his children and grandchildren. A wildlife photographer, he has written articles to accompany his photography for publications such as *The Charleston Magazine, Water Dogs, Bloodlines,* and *Hunting and Fishing.*

Douglas Wyant, a native of Camden, lives in Kershaw County with his wife Gail. Two stories about his parents were included in Camden Writers first anthology, *Serving Up Memory,* and two of his poems were selected for Camden Poets Society 25th Anniversary Collection, *What We Keep.* He can be contacted at douglas.wyant@att.net.

Myra Yeatts retired from teaching and quickly became a full-time volunteer for various church organizations. She writes daily and enjoys the collaboration with Camden Writers. Putting pen to paper has been a lifelong practice and will always be a strong contender for her time. Just ask her Labradoodle who watches mournfully and sighs deeply whenever the mistress approaches the "writing chair." Yeatts has made contributions to *The Petigru Review, moonShine Review,* and *Southern Sampler.* She also wrote and performed a monologue at Sumter Little Theatre.

Acknowledgments

Without the dedication of several individuals, this anthology would still be an idea, not a reality. Thanks to all Camden Writers for their stories, poems, and recipes and to contributor Art Shealy for his photograph and story, "The Barn."

After the writers group had spent months of submitting, critiquing, and revising members' work, Kathryn Etters Lovatt and I began the process of organizing contributions into divisions and placing them into the book. We then added photographs, some submitted by members and some found in our files and on our iPhones. An exception is the picture of the four travelers on page 145. Thanks to Judy Bowers Kambeitz for capturing the moment, symbolic for all sojourners.

Several weeks passed, and at last we had proof copies, tangible evidence of progress. Four Camden Writers agreed to help us read the proofs: Douglas Wyant, Martha Dabbs Greenway, Myra Yeatts, and Brenda Bevan Remmes. Without their sharp eyes and dedication to our communal work, the anthology would be filled with errors ranging from misplaced quotation marks and misspellings to spacing errors and missing words.

We considered dozens of photographs for our cover, but nothing seemed right. Then one morning someone drove by the Robert Mills Courthouse on her way into Camden and was delighted to see what appeared to be colorful umbrellas blooming along the sidewalk and on the courthouse grounds. The driver quickly parked her car and snapped several photographs of the scenes. "It was so beautiful. I had to stop," she said.

We're glad Ann Padgett Johnson did—not only because of the vibrant colors of the blooming umbrellas but also because of what they represent—lives of loved ones touched by Hospice. The day was November 3, 2016, and the display was part of a state-wide event for National Hospice and Palliative Care Month. *Life Blooms Eternal* was the theme, and story-telling was part of the agenda.

When it got down to crunch time, Kathryn Etters Lovatt, Douglas Wyant, and I put in a lot of overtime, and we're appreciative to patient and understanding family members and friends who ignored our whining and tolerated our obsession with "the book."

J.P. Bowers

www.ingramcontent.com/pod-product-compliance
Lightning Source LLC
Chambersburg PA
CBHW060357180626
46817CB00007B/2459